Essay Collections
in International Relations

Garland Reference Library of Social Science (Vol. 45)

Introduction

One of the major forms in which scholarly research and analysis in international relations has appeared since the Second World War is the collection of essays by several authors. This may be associated with an occasion, honour a distinguished scholar, form the published record of a conference, or result from the initiative of an editor who commissions a series of original papers on a theme or problem.

In content and style these essays vary widely and include the ephemeral *pièce d'occasion*, the reflective essay, and the substantial research paper. As reviewers are fond of remarking about such collections, the quality is often uneven and the topics sometimes ill-connected. Whatever the merits of a volume as a whole, however, a particular contribution worthy of notice loses its individuality under the cover of the editor's name and the broad or uninformative title that such a book often bears.

Bibliographically, the field of international relations is not well provided for, but this category tends to suffer more than the scholarly monograph and journal article. Although there are a few serial bibliographical publications that give partial control of some aspects of the subject, there is no single work that deals adequately with the multi-author book in international relations as a whole. In addition, there are many essay collections in other fields containing one or two essays of interest to the international relations scholar that he is unlikely to discover. It is hoped that this bibliography of individual contributions will make more accessible much valuable scholarship and reflection.

This bibliography details original material on international relations since 1870 written in English and appearing in non-recurrent multi-author works published between 1945 and 1975. Most of these criteria are clearly defined, but the precise boundaries of the field of international relations are by no means universally agreed upon by scholars in this field. We have distinguished between core topics such as foreign policy, defence, and international organisation, and peripheral areas such as international economics, international law, and diplomatic history. The latter disciplines have

INTRODUCTION

their own specialised academic literatures, from which we have included only those essays that we judge to have more general relevance to the student and researcher in international relations.

Within these limits we have further selected only those essays that make an enduring and substantial contribution to the study of international relations. We have concentrated on the theoretical, analytical, and historical work that seems least likely to become out-of-date in the near future and have accordingly excluded much commentary on current events and situations. Introductions and conclusions that are substantial essays in their own right have been included.

The only recurring publications that we have included are NOMOS, the Yearbook of the American Society for Political and Legal Philosophy, and the symposia of The Conference on Science, Philosophy and Religion in Their Relation to the Democratic Way of Life. These contain interesting essays that might otherwise escape the scholar's attention. Although reprinted material has been excluded, we have in a few instances included books that have appeared previously or simultaneously as special issues of journals. In such cases the book form of publication is sometimes more readily available than the periodical form.

In addition, we have listed some items whose original publication was either obscure or ephemeral; similarly, English translations of essays originally published in a foreign language have been included. Only one book published before 1945, E. M. Earle's *Makers of Modern Strategy,* has been included, because it has become a classic.

The bibliography consists of four parts:

(1) List of essay collections. This provides full bibliographical details of the books whose partial or complete contents are found in the bibliography. The form of the bibliographical citation is designed to provide clear and easy reference from the shortened form of citation used in the

(2) Classified bibliography of individual essays. The essays have been grouped under broad subject classifications reflecting the main sub-divisions of the academic field of international relations as well as related disciplines. Each essay has been given a reference number that consists of the identifying letter of the section in which it appears and a number according to its order of appearance alphabetically by

Contents

Introduction vii
List of essay collections 1
Classified bibliography of individual essays 19
   A   Methodology, study and theory of international relations 21
   B   Simulation, gaming, game theory, computer analysis 28
   C   History of international relations 31
   D   International system, alliance, balance of power 41
   E   Actors, sovereignty, the state 47
   F   Nationalism, ethnicity, race 50
   G   Foreign policy, decision-making, internal/external linkages 53
   H   International conflict and crisis 63
   J   Non-strategic dimensions of war 69
   K   Strategic thought, deterrence theory, defence policy 76
   L   Arms control, disarmament, nuclear proliferation 84
   M   Diplomacy, bargaining, negotiation 87
   N   Communication, public opinion, propaganda, psychological aspects of international relations 91
   P   Ethics, morality, ideas, values, ideology 96
   Q   Peace and pacifism 101
   R   International law 103
   S   International organisation 113
   T   International/world order and integration 119
   U   Third world, developing areas, colonialism, non-alignment 123
   V   Area studies, regionalism, regional integration 128
   W   Economics and international politics 133
   X   Science and technology 136
Author index 139
Subject index 153

Essay Collections
in International Relations
A Classified Bibliography

Moorhead Wright
Jane Davis
and
Michael Clarke

Garland Publishing, Inc., New York & London

1977

Copyright © 1977
by Moorhead Wright, Jane Davis,
and Michael Clarke

All Rights Reserved

Library of Congress Cataloging in Publication Data

Wright, Moorhead.
    Essay collections in international relations.

    (Garland reference library of social science ; v. 45)
    Includes indexes.
    1. International relations--Bibliography. I. Davis,
Jane, 1950-   joint author. II. Clarke, Michael,
1950-   joint author. III. Title.
Z6461.W7   [JX1315]   016.327   76-52692
ISBN 0-8240-9868-4

Printed in the United States of America

INTRODUCTION

author in the section. In those cases where the essay's title does not sufficiently indicate its contents, the title has been supplemented by a descriptive phrase in brackets. Where possible we have placed related sections together, so that the reader should also look through sections adjacent to the one in which he is principally interested. A further means of cross-reference is provided by the two indices:

(3) Author index. The reference number of each essay has been entered under its author's name. Thus the reader can look up the essays written by those scholars who are specialists in the field in which he is interested.

(4) Subject index. The reference number of each essay has been entered under the principal themes and subject matter with which it deals. In most cases the essay has not been indexed under the heading that corresponds to the classification section in which it is placed; this would have produced several excessively long index entries and would have served no useful purpose.

This bibliography has been prepared with the cooperation of several libraries, but we particularly wish to thank Chris Chadwick, David Jones, Kathy Hamilton, and other staff of the Llandinam Library, University College of Wales, for their helpfulness and advice. We also wish to thank our colleagues in the Department of International Politics for their support and suggestions.

M.W.
Aberystwyth, Wales
January 1977

LIST OF ESSAY COLLECTIONS

Brothers, New York and London.

Bryson, L., Finkelstein, L., and MacIver, R.M., eds. (1947a). Conflicts of Power in Modern Culture. New York: The Conference on Science, Philosophy and Religion in Their Relation to the Democratic Way of Life, Inc.; distributed by Harper and Brothers, New York and London.

Bryson, L., Finkelstein, L., MacIver, R.M., and McKeon, R., eds. (1953). Freedom and Authority in Our Time. New York: The Conference on Science, Philosophy and Religion in Their Relation to the Democratic Way of Life, Inc.; distributed by Harper and Brothers, New York and London.

Bryson, L., Finkelstein, L., MacIver, R.M., and McKeon, R., eds. (1954). Symbols and Values: An Initial Study. New York: The Conference on Science, Philosophy and Religion in Their Relation to the Democratic Way of Life, Inc.; distributed by Harper and Brothers, New York and London.

Buchan, A., ed. (1966). A World of Nuclear Powers? Englewood Cliffs, N.J.: Prentice-Hall.

Buehrig, E.H., ed. (1966). Essays in Political Science. Bloomington and London: Indiana University Press.

Burns, R.D., and Bennett, E.M., eds. (1974). Diplomats in Crisis: United States-Chinese-Japanese Relations, 1919-1941. Santa Barbara, Calif.: American Bibliographical Center--Clio Press; Oxford: European Bibliographical Center--Clio Press.

Burton, J.W., ed. (1966). Nonalignment. London: Andre Deutsch.

Butterfield, H., and Wight, M., eds. (1966). Diplomatic Investigations: Essays in the Theory of International Politics. London: George Allen and Unwin.

Butwell, R., ed. (1969). Foreign Policy and the Developing Nation. Lexington: University of Kentucky Press.

Cantril, H., ed. (1950). Tensions that Cause Wars. Urbana: University of Illinois Press.

Carlton, D., and Schaerf, C., eds. (1975). The Dynamics of the Arms Race. London: Croom Helm.

Carlton, D., and Schaerf, C., eds. (1975a). International Terrorism and World Security. London: Croom Helm.

Charlesworth, J.C., ed. (1967). Contemporary Political Analysis. New York: The Free Press; London: Collier-Macmillan.

Confino, M., and Shimon, S., eds. (1973). *The U.S.S.R. and the Middle East*. Jerusalem: Israel Universities Press.

Coplin, W.D., ed. (1968). *Simulation in the Study of Politics*. Chicago: Markham.

Corbet, H., and Jackson, R., eds. (1974). *In Search of a New World Economic Order*. London: Croom Helm.

Cordier, A.W., ed. (1971). *Columbia Essays in International Affairs*, vol. VI. New York and London: Columbia University Press.

Cox, R.W., and Jacobson, H.K., eds. (1973). *The Anatomy of Influence: Decision-Making in International Organisation*. New Haven and London: Yale University Press.

Craig, G.A., and Gilbert, F., eds. (1953). *The Diplomats 1919-1939*. Princeton, N.J.: Princeton University Press. (Reprinted in two paperback volumes by Atheneum, New York, in 1963, with same pagination.)

Crawford, E.T., and Biderman, A.D., eds. (1969). *Social Scientists and International Affairs: A Case for a Sociology of Social Science*. New York and London: John Wiley.

DeConde, A., ed. (1957). *Isolation and Security: Ideas and Interests in Twentieth-Century American Foreign Policy*. Durham, N.C.: Duke University Press.

De Reuck, A., and Knight, J., eds. (1966). *Conflict in Society*. London: J. & A. Churchill.

Deutsch, K., and Hoffmann, S., eds. (1971). *The Relevance of International Law*. Garden City, N.Y.: Doubleday (Anchor Books). (Originally published in hardcover by Schenkman in 1968, with different pagination)

Earle, E.M., ed. (1941). *Makers of Modern Strategy*. Princeton, N.J.: Princeton University Press; London: Oxford University Press.

Earle, E.M., ed. (1950). *Nationalism and Internationalism: Essays Inscribed to Carlton J.H. Hayes*. New York: Columbia University Press.

Eissenstat, B.W., ed. (1975). *The Soviet Union: The Seventies and Beyond*. Lexington, Mass.: Lexington Books.

Engel, S., ed. (1964). *Law, State, and International Legal Order: Essays in Honor of Hans Kelsen*. Knoxville: University of Tennessee Press.

Erickson, J., Crowley, E.L., and Galay, N., eds. (1966). The Military-Technical Revolution. London: Pall Mall.

Falk, R.A., ed. (1971). The International Law of Civil War. Baltimore and London: The Johns Hopkins Press.

Falk, R.A., and Black, C.E., eds. (1969). The Future of the International Legal Order, vol. I, Trends and Patterns. Princeton, N.J.: Princeton University Press.

Falk, R.A., and Black, C.E., eds. (1970). The Future of the International Legal Order, vol. II, Wealth and Resources. Princeton, N.J.: Princeton University Press.

Farrell, J.C., and Smith, A.P., eds. (1967). Image and Reality in World Politics. New York and London: Columbia University Press.

Farrell, J.C., and Smith, A.P., eds. (1968). Theory and Reality in International Relations. New York and London: Columbia University Press.

Farrell, R.B., ed. (1966). Approaches to Comparative and International Politics. Evanston, Ill.: Northwestern University Press.

Fawcett, J.E.S., and Higgins, R., eds. (1974). International Organisation: Law in Movement. Essays in Honour of John McMahon. London and New York: Oxford University Press.

Fisher, R., ed. (1964). International Conflict and Behavioral Science: The Craigville Papers. New York: Basic Books.

Fletcher, R., ed. (1974). The Science of Society and the Unity of Mankind: A Memorial Volume for Morris Ginsberg. London: Heinemann Educational.

Fox, W.T.R., ed. (1959). Theoretical Aspects of International Relations. Notre Dame, Ind.: University of Notre Dame Press.

Franck, T.M., and Weisband, E., eds. (1974). Secrecy and Foreign Policy. New York and London: Oxford University Press.

French, P.A., ed. (1972). Individual and Collective Responsibility: Massacre at My Lai. Cambridge, Mass.: Schenkman.

French, P.A., ed. (1974). Conscientious Actions: The Revelation of the Pentagon Papers. Cambridge Mass.: Schenkman.

Fried, M., Harris, M., and Murphy, R., eds. (1967). War: The Anthropology of Armed Conflict and Aggression. New York: The Natural History Press.

Friedman, J.R., Bladen, C., and Rosen, S., eds. (1970). Alliance in International Politics. Boston: Allyn and Bacon.

Friedmann, W., Henkin, L., and Lissitzyn, O.J., eds. (1972). Transnational Law in a Changing Society: Essays in Honor of Philip C. Jessup. New York and London: Columbia University Press.

Friedrich, C.J., ed. (1958). Authority. Cambridge, Mass.: Harvard University Press. (NOMOS I)

Friedrich, C.J., ed. (1969). Revolution. New York: Atherton. (NOMOS VIII)

Gatzke, H.W., ed. (1972). European Diplomacy Between Two Wars, 1919-1939. Chicago: Quadrangle.

Gifford, P., and Louis, W.R., eds. (1967). Britain and Germany in Africa. New Haven and London: Yale University Press.

Gifford, P., and Louis, W.R., eds. (1971). France and Britain in Africa. New Haven and London: Yale University Press.

Gilbert, F., and Graubard, S.R., eds. (1972). Historical Studies Today. New York: W.W. Norton.

Gilbert, J.H., ed. (1973). The New Era in American Foreign Policy. New York: St. Martin's.

Gilbert, M., ed. (1966). A Century of Conflict: Essays for A.J.P. Taylor. London: Hamish Hamilton.

Ginsberg, R., ed. (1969). The Critique of War: Contemporary Philosophical Explorations. Chicago: Henry Regnery.

Goldwin, R.A., ed. (1963). America Armed: Essays on United States Military Policy. Chicago: Rand McNally.

Goodwin, G.L., and Linklater, A., eds. (1975). New Dimensions of World Politics. London: Croom Helm.

Gordenker, L., ed. (1971). The United Nations in International Politics. Princeton, N.J.: Princeton University Press.

Gray, R.B., ed. (1969). International Security Systems: Concepts and Models of World Order. Itasca, Ill.: F.E. Peacock.

Graymer, L., ed. (1971). Systems and Actors in International Politics. Scranton, Pa.: Chandler.

Greenstein, F.I., and Polsby, N.W., eds. (1975). Handbook of Political Science, vols. 6 and 8. Reading, Mass., and London: Addison-Wesley.

Gregg, R.W., ed. (1968). International Organization in the Western Hemisphere. Syracuse: Syracuse University Press.

Grob, G.N., ed. (1967). Statesmen and Statecraft of the Modern West. Barre, Mass.: Barre Publishers.

Groom, A.J.R., and Taylor, P., eds. (1975). Functionalism: Theory and Practice in International Relations. London: University of London Press.

Gross, L., ed. (1967). Sociological Theory: Inquiries and Paradigms. New York, Evanston, Ill., and London: Harper and Row.

Guetzkow, H., et al. eds. (1963). Simulation in International Relations: Developments for Research and Teaching. Englewood Cliffs, N.J.: Prentice-Hall.

Gurian, W., and Fitzsimons, M.A., eds. (1954). The Catholic Church in World Affairs. Notre Dame, Ind.: University of Notre Dame Press.

Haas, M., ed. (1974). International Systems: A Behavioral Approach. New York and London: Chandler.

Haas, M., and Kariel, H.S., eds. (1970). Approaches to the Study of Political Science. Scranton, Pa.: Chandler.

Hanrieder, W.F., ed. (1971). Comparative Foreign Policy: Theoretical Essays. New York: David McKay.

Harrison, H.V., ed. (1964). The Role of Theory in International Relations. Princeton, N.J.: D. Van Nostrand.

Hatton, R., and Anderson, M.S., eds. (1970). Studies in Diplomatic History: Essays in Memory of David Bayne Horn. London: Longman.

Hekhuis, D.J., McClintock, C.G., and Burns, A.L., eds. (1964). International Stability: Military, Economic and Political Dimensions. New York and London: John Wiley.

Held, V., Morgenbesser, S., and Nagel, T., eds. (1974). Philosophy, Morality and International Affairs. New York and London: Oxford University Press.

Hermann, C.F., ed. (1972). International Crises: Insights from Behavioral Research. New York: The Free Press; London: Collier-Macmillan.

Hilsman, R., and Good, R.C., eds. (1965). Foreign Policy in the Sixties: The Issues and the Instruments. Essays in Honor of Arnold Wolfers. Baltimore: The Johns Hopkins Press.

Hoffman, A.S., ed. (1968). International Communication and the New Diplomacy. Bloomington and London: Indiana University Press.

Hoffmann, E.P., and Fleron, F.J., eds. (1971). The Conduct of Soviet Foreign Policy. London: Butterworths.

Hoffmann, S., ed. (1968). Conditions of World Order. Boston: Houghton Mifflin.

Hoffmann, S., et al. (1963). In Search of France. New York: Harper and Row.

Holbraad, C., ed. (1971). Super Powers and World Order. Canberra: Australian National University Press.

Horton, F.B., Rogerson, A.C. and Warner, E.L., eds. (1974). Comparative Defense Policy. Baltimore and London: The Johns Hopkins University Press.

Howard, M., ed. (1965). The Theory and Practice of War: Essays Presented to Captain B.H. Liddell Hart. London: Cassell.

Ingham, K., ed. (1974). Foreign Relations of African States. London: Butterworths.

International Peace Research Association (1966). Proceedings of the International Peace Research Association Inaugural Conference. Assen, Netherlands: Van Gorcum.

Ionescu, G., ed. (1974). Between Sovereignty and Integration. London: Croom Helm.

Irish, M.D., ed. (1968). Political Science: Advance of the Discipline. Englewood Cliffs, N.J.: Prentice-Hall.

Iriye, Akira, ed. (1975). Mutual Images: Essays in American-Japanese Relations. Cambridge, Mass., and London: Harvard University Press.

Jacob, P.E., and Toscano, J.V., eds. (1964). The Integration of Political Communities. Philadelphia and New York: J.B. Lippincott.

James, A., ed. (1973). The Bases of International Order: Essays in Honour of C.A.W. Manning. London and New York: Oxford University Press.

Jaquet, L.G.M., ed. (1971). Intervention in International Politics. The Hague: Netherlands Institute of International Affairs.

Jenks, C.W., et al. (1963). International Law in a Changing World. Dobbs Ferry, N.Y.: Oceana.

John, I.G., ed. (1975). EEC Policy Towards Eastern Europe.
Farnborough, Hants.: Saxon House; Lexington, Mass.: Lexington Books.

Johnson, E.A.J., ed. (1964). The Dimensions of Diplomacy.
Baltimore: The Johns Hopkins Press.

Jordan, R.S., ed. (1971). International Administration: Its Evolution and Contemporary Applications. New York and London: Oxford University Press.

Jordan, R.S., ed. (1972). Multinational Cooperation: Economic, Social and Scientific Development. New York and London: Oxford University Press.

Kaiser, K., and Morgan, R., eds. (1971). Britain and West Germany: Changing Societies and the Future of Foreign Policy. London and New York: Oxford University Press.

Kamenka, E., ed. (1973). Nationalism: The Nature and Evolution of an Idea. Canberra: Australian National University Press.

Kaplan, M.A., ed. (1962). The Revolution in World Politics. New York and London: John Wiley.

Kaplan, M.A., ed. (1968). New Approaches to International Relations. New York: St. Martin's.

Kaplan, M.A., ed. (1973). Strategic Thinking and Its Moral Implications. Chicago: University of Chicago Press.

Kelman, H.C., ed. (1965). International Behavior: A Social-Psychological Analysis. New York and London: Holt, Rinehart and Winston.

Keohane, R.O., and Nye, J.S., eds. (1972). Transnational Relations and World Politics. Cambridge, Mass.: Harvard University Press.

Kilson, M., ed. (1975). New States in the Modern World. Cambridge, Mass., and London: Harvard University Press.

Kitagawa, J.M., ed. (1969). Understanding Modern China. Chicago: Quadrangle.

Knorr, K., and Read, T., eds. (1962). Limited Strategic War. London: Pall Mall.

Knorr, K., and Rosenau, J.N., eds. (1969). Contending Approaches to International Politics. Princeton, N.J.: Princeton University Press.

Knorr, K., and Verba, S., eds. (1961). The International System: Theoretical Essays. Princeton, N.J.: Princeton University Press.

Koch, H.W., ed. (1972). The Origins of the First World War: Great Power Rivalry and German War Aims. London: Macmillan.

Kohnstamm, M., and Wolfgang, H., eds. (1973). A Nation Writ Large?: Foreign-Policy Problems Before the European Community. London: Macmillan.

Krieger, L., and Stern, F., eds. (1968). The Responsibility of Power: Historical Essays in Honor of Hajo Holborn. London: Macmillan, 1968; New York: Doubleday, 1967.

Kriesberg, L., ed. (1968). Social Processes in International Relations: A Reader. New York and London: John Wiley.

Kuntz, P.G., ed. (1968). The Concept of Order. Seattle and London: University of Washington Press.

Lasswell, H.D., and Cleveland, H., eds. (1962). The Ethic of Power: The Interplay of Religion, Philosophy, and Politics. New York: Conference on Science, Philosophy and Religion in Their Relation to the Democratic Way of Life; Distributed by Harper and Brothers, New York.

Laszlo, E., ed. (1973). The World System: Models, Norms, Applications. New York: George Braziller.

Lederer, I.J., ed. (1962). Russian Foreign Policy: Essays in Historical Perspective. New Haven and London: Yale University Press.

Lee, D.E., and McReynolds, G.E., eds. (1949). Essays in History and International Relations: In Honor of George Hubbard Blakeslee. Worcester, Mass.: Clark University.

Lefever, E.W., ed. (1972). Ethics and World Politics: Four Perspectives. Baltimore and London: The Johns Hopkins University Press.

Leifer, M., ed. (1972). Constraints and Adjustments in British Foreign Policy. London: George Allen and Unwin.

Lepawsky, A., Buehrig, E.H., and Lasswell, H.D., eds. (1971). The Search for World Order: Studies by Students and Colleagues of Quincy Wright. New York: Appleton-Century-Crofts.

Lerner, D., and Lasswell, H.D., eds. (1951). The Policy Sciences. Stanford, Calif.: Stanford University Press.

Lindberg, L.N., and Scheingold, S.A., eds. (1971). Regional Integration: Theory and Research. Cambridge, Mass.: Harvard University Press.

Lipsky, G.A., ed. (1953). Law and Politics in the World Community: Essays on Hans Kelsen's Pure Theory and Related Problems in International Law. Berkeley and Los Angeles: University of California Press.

Loewenheim, F.L., ed. (1967). The Historian and the Diplomat: The Role of History and Historians in American Foreign Policy. New York, Evanston, Ill., and London: Harper and Row.

London, K., ed. (1963). New Nations in a Divided World. New York and London: Praeger.

Long, E.L., Jr., and Handy, R.T., eds. (1970). Theology and Church in Times of Change. Philadelphia: The Westminster Press.

Luard, E., ed. (1972). The International Regulation of Civil Wars. London: Thames and Hudson.

MacKinnon, D.M., ed. (1969). Making Moral Decisions. London: S.P.C.K.

Macridis, R.C., ed. (1972). Foreign Policy in World Politics. 4th Ed. Englewood Cliffs, N.J.: Prentice-Hall.

MccGwire, M., ed. (1973). Soviet Naval Developments: Capability and Context. New York and London: Praeger.

McKay, V., ed. (1966). African Diplomacy: Studies in the Determinants of Foreign Policy. London: Pall Mall.

McNeil, E.B., ed. (1965). The Nature of Human Conflict. Englewood Cliffs, N.J.: Prentice-Hall.

McWhinney, E., ed. (1964). Law, Foreign Policy, and the East-West Détente. Toronto: University of Toronto Press.

Medlicott, W.N., ed. (1963). From Metternich to Hitler: Aspects of British and Foreign History 1814-1939. New York: Barnes and Noble.

Mélanges Raymond Aron (1971). Science et conscience de la société: Mélanges en l'honneur de Raymond Aron. Paris: Calmann-Levy. Two volumes.

Mélanges Pierre Renouvin (1966). Études d'histoire des relations internationales. Paris: Presses Universitaires de France.

Mendlovitz, S.H., ed. (1975). On the Creation of a Just World Order: Preferred Worlds for the 1990's. New York: The Free Press.

Merritt, R.L., ed. (1972). Communication in International Politics. Chicago and London: University of Illinois Press.

Merritt, R.L., and Puchala, D.J., eds. (1968). Western European Perspectives on International Affairs: Public Opinion Studies and Evaluations. New York and London: Praeger.

Moore, J.N., ed. (1974). Law and Civil War in the Modern World. Baltimore and London: The Johns Hopkins University Press.

Morgan, R., ed. (1972). The Study of International Affairs: Essays in Honour of Kenneth Younger. London and New York: Oxford University Press.

Mudd, S., ed. (1967). Conflict Resolution and World Education. Bloomington and London: Indiana University Press.

Nagle, W.J., ed. (1960). Morality and Modern Warfare. Baltimore: Helican.

Northedge, F.S., ed. (1974). The Foreign Policies of the Powers. 2nd Ed. London: Faber and Faber.

Northedge, F.S., ed. (1974a). The Use of Force in International Relations. London: Faber and Faber; New York: The Free Press.

Northrop, F.S.C., ed (1949). Ideological Differences and World Order : Studies in the Philosophy and Science of the World's Cultures. New Haven and London: Yale University Press.

Ogburn, W.F., ed. (1949). Technology and International Relations. Chicago: University of Chicago Press.

Palmer, N.D., ed. (1970). A Design for International Relations Research: Scope, Theory, Methods and Relevance. Philadelphia: The American Academy of Political and Social Science. (Monograph 10)

Parekh, B., and Berki, R.N., eds. (1972). The Morality of Politics. London: George Allen and Unwin.

Parel, A., ed. (1972). The Political Calculus: Essays on Machiavelli's Philosophy. Toronto: University of Toronto Press.

Pear, T.H., ed. (1950). Psychological Factors of Peace and War. London and New York: Hutchinson.

Pelczynski, Z.A., ed. (1971). Hegel's Political Philosophy: Problems and Perspectives. Cambridge: Cambridge University Press.

Pennock, J.R., and Chapman, J.W., eds. (1967). Equality. New York: Atherton. (NOMOS IX)

Pennock, J.R., and Chapman, J.W., eds. (1972). Coercion. Chicago: Aldine-Atherton. (NOMOS XIV)

Penrose, E.F., Lyon, P., and Penrose, E., eds. (1970). New Orientations: Essays in International Relations. London: Frank Cass.

Plischke, E., ed. (1964). Systems of Integrating the International Community. Princeton, N.J.: D. Van Nostrand.

Pool, I. de S., Schramm, W., et al., eds. (1973). Handbook of Communication. Chicago: Rand McNally.

Porter, B., ed. (1972). The Aberystwyth Papers: International Politics 1919-1969. London and New York: Oxford University Press.

Proctor, J.H., ed. (1965). Islam and International Relations. London: Pall Mall.

Pruitt, D.G., and Snyder, R.C., eds. (1969). Theory and Research on the Causes of War. Englewood Cliffs, N.J.: Prentice-Hall.

Quester, G.H., ed. (1975). Sea Power in the 1970s. New York and London: Dunellen.

Rajan, M.S., ed. (1971). Studies in Politics: National and International. Prepared in Honour of Dr. A. Appadorai. Delhi, Bombay, and Bangalore: Vikas.

Ranney, A., ed. (1962). Essays on the Behavioral Study of Politics. Urbana, Ill.: University of Illinois Press.

Raphael, D.D., ed. (1967). Political Theory and the Rights of Man. London: Macmillan.

Rapoport, A., ed. (1974). Game Theory as a Theory of Conflict Resolution. Boston: D. Reidel.

Reigersman-van der Eerden, A.M.C.H., and Zoon, G., eds. (1974). A Desirable World: Essays in Honor of Professor Bart Landheer. The Hague: Martinus Nijhoff.

Ridley, F.F., ed. (1975). Studies in Politics. Oxford: Clarendon Press.

Riggs, F.W., ed. (1971). International Studies: Present Status and Future Prospects. Philadelphia: The American Academy of Political and Social Science. (Monograph 12)

Robson, W.A., ed. (1972). Man and the Social Sciences. London: George Allen and Unwin.

Rogow, A.A., ed. (1969). Politics, Personality and Social Science in the Twentieth Century: Essays in Honour of Harold D. Lasswell. Chicago and London: University of Chicago Press.

Rosen, S., ed. (1973). Testing the Theory of the Military-Industrial Complex. Lexington, Mass.: Lexington Books.

Rosenau, J.N., ed. (1961). International Politics and Foreign Policy: A Reader in Research and Theory. New York: The Free Press.

Rosenau, J.N., ed. (1964). International Aspects of Civil Strife. Princeton, N.J.: Princeton University Press.

Rosenau, J.N., ed. (1967). Domestic Sources of Foreign Policy. New York: The Free Press; London: Collier-Macmillan.

Rosenau, J.N., ed. (1969). International Politics and Foreign Policy. 2nd ed. New York: The Free Press; London: Collier-Macmillan.

Rosenau, J.N., ed. (1969a). Linkage Politics: Essays on the Convergence of National and International Systems. New York: The Free Press; London: Collier-Macmillan.

Rosenau, J.N., ed. (1974). Comparing Foreign Policies: Theories, Findings, and Methods. New York: Sage and John Wiley.

Rosenau, J.N., Davis, V., and East, M.A., eds. (1972). The Analysis of International Politics: Essays in Honor of Harold and Margaret Sprout. New York: The Free Press; London: Collier-Macmillan.

Roth, J.J., ed. (1967). World War I: A Turning Point in Modern History. New York: Knopf.

Rubinstein, A.Z., ed. (1975). Soviet and Chinese Influence in the Third World. New York, Washington and London: Praeger.

Russett, B.M., ed. (1972). Peace, War, and Numbers. Beverly Hills, Calif., and London: Sage.

Said, A.A., ed. (1968). Theory of International Relations: The Crisis of Relevance. Englewood Cliffs, N.J.: Prentice-Hall.

Sarkesian, S.C., ed. (1972). The Military-Industrial Complex: A Reassessment. Beverly Hills, Calif., and London: Sage.

Sarkissian, A.O., ed. (1961). Studies in Diplomatic History and Historiography in Honour of G.P. Gooch. London: Longmans.

Scheinman, L., and Wilkinson, D., eds. (1968). International Law and Political Crisis: An Analytical Casebook. Boston: Little, Brown.

Schou, A., and Brundtland, A.O., eds. (1971). Small States in International Relations. New York and London: John Wiley; Stockholm: Almqvist and Wiksell.

Shepherd, G.W., Jr., ed. (1970). Racial Influences on American Foreign Policy. New York and London: Basic Books.

Shepherd, G.W., Jr., and LeMelle, T.J., eds. (1970). Race Among Nations: A Conceptual Approach. Lexington, Mass: D.C. Heath.

Shubik, M., ed. (1964). Game Theory and Related Approaches to Social Behavior. New York and London: John Wiley.

Simpson, S., ed. (1972). Instruction in Diplomacy: The Liberal Arts Approach. Philadelphia: The American Academy of Political and Social Science. (Monograph 13)

Singer, J.D., ed. (1968). Quantitative International Politics: Insights and Evidence. New York: The Free Press; London: Collier-Macmillan.

Small, M., ed. (1970). Public Opinion and Historians. Detroit: Wayne State University Press.

Speigel, S.L., and Waltz, K.N., eds. (1971). Conflict in World Politics. Cambridge, Mass.: Winthrop.

Sperrazzo, G., ed. (1965). Psychology and International Relations. Washington, D.C.: Georgetown University Press.

Stankiewicz, W.J., ed. (1969). In Defence of Sovereignty. New York and London: Oxford University Press.

Stoessinger, J.G., and Westin, A.F., eds. (1964). Power and Order: 6 Cases in World Politics. New York: Harcourt, Brace and World.

Tanter, R., and Ullman, R.H., eds. (1972). Theory and Policy in International Relations. Princeton, N.J.: Princeton University Press.

Thompson, L., and Butler, J., eds. (1975). Change in Contemporary South Africa. Berkeley and Los Angeles: University of California Press.

Tiselius, A., and Nilsson, S., eds. (1970). The Place of Value in a World of Facts. New York and London: John Wiley; Stockholm: Almqvist and Wiksell.

Twitchett, K.J., ed. (1971). International Security: Reflections on Survival and Stability. London and New York: Oxford University Press.

Varma, B.N., ed. (1962). A New Survey of the Social Sciences. London: Asia Publishing House.

Waites, N., ed. (1971). Troubled Neighbours: Franco-British Relations in the Twentieth Century. London: Weidenfeld and Nicolson.

Wallace, V.H., ed. (1957). Paths to Peace: A Study of War, its Causes and Prevention. London and New York: Cambridge University Press.

Whitson, W.W., ed. (1972). The Military and Political Power in China in the 1970s. New York, Washington and London: Praeger.

Wiener, P.P., and Fisher, J., eds. (1974). Violence and Aggression in the History of Ideas. New Brunswick, N.J.: Rutgers University Press.

Wilson, I., ed. (1973). China and the World Community. Sydney and London: Angus Robertson.

Winter, J.M., ed. (1975). War and Economic Development: Essays in Memory of David Joslin. Cambridge: Cambridge University Press.

Wolfers, A., et al. (1966). The United States in a Disarmed World. Baltimore: The Johns Hopkins Press.

Wolman, B.B., ed. (1973). The Psychoanalytic Interpretation of History. New York and London: Harper and Row.

Wood, R.S., ed. (1971). The Process of International Organization. New York: Random House.

Woodward, E.L., et al. (1949). Foundations for World Order. Denver: University of Denver Press.

Wright, Q., ed. (1948). The World Community. Chicago: University of Chicago Press.

Wright, Q., Evan, W.M., and Deutsch, M., eds. (1962). Preventing World War III: Some Proposals. New York: Simon and Schuster.

CLASSIFIED BIBLIOGRAPHY OF

INDIVIDUAL ESSAYS

A - METHODOLOGY, STUDY AND THEORY OF INTERNATIONAL RELATIONS

A1   Alger, C.F., "Trends in International Relations Research", in Palmer (1970), 7-28.

A2   Alker, H.R., "The Long Road to International Relations Theory: Problems of Statistical Nonadditivity", in Kaplan (1968), 137-169.

A3   Aron, R., "Theory and Theories in International Relations: A Conceptual Analysis", in Palmer (1970), 55-66.

A4   Aron, R., "What is a Theory of International Relations?", in Farrell and Smith (1968), 1-22.

A5   Benson, O., "Challenges for Research in International Relations and Comparative Politics", in Farrell (1966), 338-358.

A6   Bobrow, D.B., "The Relevance Potential of Different Products [of international relations theory]", in Tanter and Ullman (1972), 204-228.

A7   Brody, R.A., "Convergences and Challenges in International Relations", in Riggs (1971), 172-188.

A8   Brody, R.A., "International Relations As A Behavioral Science: Problems, Approaches and Findings", in Sperrazzo (1965), 53-61.

A9   Brody, R.A., "The Study of International Politics qua Science: The Emphasis on Methods and Techniques", in Knorr and Rosenau (1969), 110-128.

A10 Bull, H., "The Theory of International Politics, 1919-1969", in Porter (1972), 30-55.

A11 Bundy, M., "The Battlefields of Power and the Searchlights of the Academy", in Johnson (1964), 1-15.

A12 Burns, A.L., "Prospects for a General Theory of International Relations", in Knorr and Verba (1961), 25-46.

A13 Burns, A.L., "Quantitative Approaches to International Relations", in Kaplan (1968), 170-201.

A14 Burns, A.L., "Scientific and Strategic-Political Theories of International Politics", in Porter (1972), 56-85.

A15   Burrowes, R., "Mirror, Mirror, on the Wall....: A Comparison of Event Data Sources", in Rosenau (1974), 383-406.

A16   Deutsch, K., "Problem Solving in international relations : The Behavioral Approach", in Hoffman (1968), 64-88.

A17   Fisher, R., "International Relations Theory and the Policy Maker", in Said (1968), 43-58.

A18   Fox, W.T.R., "Harold D. Lasswell and the Study of World Politics: Configurative Analysis, Garrison State, and World Commonwealth", in Rogow (1969), 367-381.

A19   Fox, W.T.R., "Theories as Forces in Modern World Politics", in Harrison (1964), 75-98.

A20   Fox, W.T.R., "The Use of International Relations Theory", in Fox (1959), 29-49.

A21   Freyre, G., "Internationalizing Social Science", in Cantril (1950), 139-165.

A22   Galtung, J., "Small Group Theory and the Theory of International Relations: A Study in Isomorphism", in Kaplan (1968), 270-302.

A23   Galtung, J., "The Social Sciences: An Essay on Polarization and Integration", in Knorr and Rosenau (1969), 243-285.

A24   Goodwin, G.L., "Conflict and Co-operation [the study of International Relations at the London School of Economics]", in Robson (1972), 89-110.

A25   Haas, M., "The Future of International Relations Theory", in Haas (1974), 351-376.

A26   Haas, M., "International Relations Theory", in Haas and Kariel (1970), 444-476.

A27   Haas, M., "A Plea for Bridge Building in International Relations", in Knorr and Rosenau (1969), 158-176.

A28   Haas, M., "The Scope and Method of International Relations", in Haas (1974), 1-49.

A29   Harrison, H.V., "Introduction [to the role of theory in international relations]", in Harrison (1964), 1-14.

A30   Hoggard, G.D., "Differential Source Coverage in Foreign Policy Analysis", in Rosenau (1974), 353-382.

A31   Hoole, F.W., "The Behavioral Science Orientation to the Study of International Administration", in Jordan (1972), 327-364.

A32   Jervis, R., "The Costs of the Quantitative Study of International Relations", in Knorr and Rosenau (1969), 177-217.

A33   John, I.G., Garnett, J.C., and Wright, M., "International Politics at Aberystwyth, 1919-1969", in Porter (1972), 86-102.

A34   Kahn, H., "The Alternative World Futures Approach", in Kaplan (1968), 83-136.

A35   Kaplan, M.A., "The New Great Debate: Traditionalism vs. Science in International Relations", in Knorr and Rosenau (1969), 39-61.

A36   Kaplan, M.A., "Problems of Theory Building and Theory Confirmation in International Politics", in Knorr and Verba (1961), 6-24.

A37   Kaplan, M.A., "Traditionalism vs. Science in International Relations", in Kaplan (1968), 1-18.

A38   Kelman, H.C., "Social-Psychological Approaches to the Study of International Relations: Definition of Scope", in Kelman (1965), 3-39.

A39   Kelman, H.C., "Social-Psychological Approaches to the Study of International Relations: The Question of Relevance", in Kelman (1965), 565-607.

A40   Kindleberger, C.P., "International Political Theory from Outside", in Fox (1959), 69-82.

A41   Knorr, K., and Rosenau, J.N., "Tradition and Science in the Study of International Politics", in Knorr and Rosenau (1969), 3-19.

A42   Landheer, B., "The Sociological Approach to International Relations", in Bains (1961), 77-90.

A43   Lasswell, H.D., "The Cross-Disciplinary Manifold: The Chicago Prototype", in Lepawsky, Buehrig and Lasswell (1971), 416-428.

A44   Lepawsky, A., "Concerning Quincy Wright", in Lepawsky, Buehrig and Lasswell (1971), xi-xx.

A45   Levy, M.J., "'Does it Matter if He's Naked?' Bawled the Child [on the methodological debate between behavioralists and traditionalists]", in Knorr and Rosenau (1969), 87-109.

A46   Lyon, P., "The Great Globe Itself: Continuity and Change", in Penrose, Lyon and Penrose (1970), 1-27.

A47   McClelland, C.A., "Field Theory and System Theory in International Relations", in Lepawsky, Buehrig and Lasswell (1971), 371-385.

A48   McClelland, C.A., "International Relations: Wisdom or Science?", in Rosenau (1969), 3-5.

A49   McGowan, P.J., "A Bayesian Approach to the Problems of Events Data Validity", in Rosenau (1974), 407-433.

A50   Morgan, R., "E.H. Carr and the Study of International Relations", in Abramsky (1974), 171-180.

A51   Morgan, R., "The Study of International Politics", in Morgan (1972), 271-291.

A52   Morgenthau, H.J., "Common Sense and Theories of International Relations", in Farrell and Smith (1968), 23-30.

A53   Morgenthau, H.J., "The Intellectual and Political Functions of a Theory of International Relations", in Harrison (1964), 99-118.

A54   Morgenthau, H.J., "The Nature and Limits of a Theory of International Relations", in Fox (1959), 15-28.

A55   Naroll, R., "Scientific Comparative Politics and International Relations", in Farrell (1966), 329-337.

A56   Nitze, P.A., "Necessary and Sufficient Elements of a General Theory of International Relations", in Fox (1959), 1-14.

A57   North, R.C., "The Behavior of Nation-States: Problems of Conflict and Integration", in Kaplan (1968), 303-356.

A58   North, R.C., "Research Pluralism and the International Elephant", in Knorr and Rosenau (1969), 218-242.

A59   Olson, W.C., "The Growth of a Discipline [of international politics 1919-1969]", in Porter (1972), 3-29.

A60   Padover, S.K., "International Relations", in Varma (1962), 21-29.

A61 Puchala, D.J., "Factor Analysis in International Survey Research", in Merritt and Puchala (1968), 142-172.

A62 Ransom, H.H. "International Relations", in Irish (1968), 55-81.

A63 Rapoport, A., "The Use of Theory in the Study of Politics", in Buehrig (1966), 3-36.

A64 Russett, B.M., "International Behavior Research: Case Studies and Cumulation", in Haas and Kariel (1970), 425-443.

A65 Russett, B.M., "A Macroscopic View of International Politics", in Rosenau, Davis and East (1972), 109-124.

A66 Russett, B.M., "Methodological and Theoretical Schools in International Relations", in Palmer (1970), 87-105.

A67 Said, A.A., "Recent Theories of International Relations: An Overview", in Said (1968), 18-25.

A68 Shonfield, A., "Introduction: The Nature of International Studies", in Morgan (1972), 1-16.

A69 Singer, J.D., "The Incompleat Theorist: Insight Without Evidence", in Knorr and Rosenau (1969), 62-86.

A70 Singer, J.D., "Knowledge, Practice, and the Social Sciences in International Politics", in Palmer (1970), 137-149.

A71 Singer, J.D., "The Level-of-Analysis Problem in International Relations", in Knorr and Verba (1961), 77-92.

A72 Singer, J.D., "Theorists and Empiricists: The Two-Culture Problem in International Politics", in Rosenau, Davis and East (1972), 80-95.

A73 Skolimowski, H., "The Twilight of Physical Descriptions and the Ascent of Normative Models", in Laszlo (1973), 97-118.

A74 Snyder, R.C., "Some Recent Trends in International Relations Theory and Research", in Ranney (1962), 103-171.

A75 Sondermann, F.A., "The Linkage between Foreign Policy and International Politics", in Rosenau (1961), 8-17.

A76 Stroup, M.J., "Some Notes on War and Peace Research", in Mudd (1967), 116-124.

A77   Tanter, R., "Explanation, Prediction and Forecasting in International Politics", in Rosenau, Davis and East (1972), 41-53.

A78   Thompson, K.W., "International Policy in War and Peace: Quincy Wright's Contribution", in Lepawsky, Buehrig and Lasswell (1971), 429-439.

A79   Thompson, K.W., "The Origins, Uses, and Problems of Theory in International Relations", in Harrison (1964), 45-73.

A80   Thompson, K.W., "Raymond Aron and the Study of International Relations", in Mélanges Raymond Aron (1971), vol. II, 385-404.

A81   Thompson, K.W., "Theory and International Studies in the Cold War", in Said (1968), 26-42.

A82   Törnebohm, H., "United Studies [of the world system]", in Laszlo (1973), 141-160.

A83   Waltz, K.N., "Theory of International Relations", in Greenstein and Polsby (1975), vol. 8, 1-85.

A84   Whitaker, U.G., Jr., "Actors, Ends, and Means: A Coarse-Screen Macro-Theory of International Relations", in Rosenau (1961), 438-448.

A85   Wight, M., "Why is There No International Theory?", in Butterfield and Wight (1966), 17-34.

A86   Wilkenfeld, J., "Models for the Analysis of Foreign Conflict Behavior of States", in Russett (1972), 275-298.

A87   Wohlstetter, A., "Theory and Opposed-Systems Design", in Kaplan (1968), 19-53.

A88   Wright, Q., "Approaches to the Understanding of International Politics", in Buehrig (1966), 61-83.

A89   Wright, Q., "Development of a General Theory of International Relations", in Harrison (1964), 15-43.

A90   Young, O.R., "[Raymond] Aron and the Whale: A Jonah in Theory", in Knorr and Rosenau (1969), 129-143.

A91   Young, O.R., "The Perils of Odysseus: On Constructing Theories in International Relations", in Tanter and Ullman (1972), 179-203.

A92   Zinnes, D.A., "Research Frontiers in the Study of International Politics", in Greenstein and Polsby (1975), vol. 8, 87-198.

A93   Zinnes, D.A., "Some Evidence Relevant to the Man-Milieu Hypothesis", in Rosenau, Davis and East (1972), 209-251.

B - SIMULATION, GAMING, GAME THEORY, COMPUTER ANALYSIS

B1   Abt, C.C., and Gorden, M., "Report on Project Temper", in Pruitt and Snyder (1969), 245-262.

B2   Alger, C.F., "Use of the Inter-Nation Simulation in Undergraduate Teaching", in Guetzkow (1963), 150-189.

B3   Alker, H.R., "Decision-Makers' Environments in the Inter-Nation Simulation", in Coplin (1968), 31-58.

B4   Benson, O., "A Simple Diplomatic Game", in Rosenau (1961), 504-511.

B5   Benson, O., "Simulation of International Relations and Diplomacy", in Borko (1962), 574-595.

B6   Bobrow, D.B., "International Interactions: Surveys and Computers", in Bobrow and Schwartz (1968), 81-110.

B7   Bobrow, D.B., and Schwartz, J.L., "Computers and International Relations", in Bobrow and Schwartz (1968), 1-19.

B8   Brody, R.A., "Varieties of Simulations in International Relations Research", in Guetzkow (1963), 190-223.

B9   Clemens, W.C., "A Propositional Analysis of the International Relations Theory in Temper [Technological, Economic, Military and Political Evaluation Routine]- A Computer Simulation of Cold War Conflict", in Coplin (1968), 59-101.

B10   Coplin, W.D., "The Impact of Simulation on Theory of International Relations", in Said (1968), 58-73.

B11   Dalkey, N.C., "Simulations and War Games", in Bobrow and Schwartz (1968), 203-213.

B12   Gorden M., "Burdens for the Designer of a Computer Simulation of International Relations: The Case of Temper", in Bobrow and Schwartz (1968), 222-243.

B13   Guetzkow, H., "Simulations in the Consolidation and Utilization of Knowledge about International Relations", in Pruitt and Snyder (1969), 284-300.

B14   Guetzkow, H., "Simulations in International Relations", in Coplin (1968), 9-30.

B15 Guetzkow, H., "Some Correspondences Between Simulations and 'Realities' in International Relations", in Kaplan (1968), 202-269.

B16 Guetzkow, H., "Structured Programs and Their Relation to Free Activity Within the Inter-Nation Simulation", in Guetzkow (1963), 103-149.

B17 Guetzkow, H., "A Use of Simulation in the Study of Inter-Nation Relations", in Guetzkow (1963), 24-38.

B18 Kaplan, M.A., "A Note on Game Theory and Bargaining", in Kaplan (1968), 483-518.

B19 Noel, R.C., "Evolution of the Inter-Nation Simulation", in Guetzkow (1963), 69-102.

B20 Noel, R.C., "Inter-Nation Simulation Participants' Manual", in Guetzkow (1963), 43-68.

B21 Quandt, R.E., "On the Use of Game Models in Theories of International Relations", in Knorr and Verba (1961), 69-76.

B22 Rapoport, A., "Introduction [to game theory as conflict resolution]", in Rapoport (1974), 1-14.

B23 Rapoport, A., "Prisoner's Dilemma - Recollections and Observations", in Rapoport (1974), 17-34.

B24 Rummel, R.J., "International Pattern and Nation Profile Delineation", in Bobrow and Schwartz (1968), 154-202.

B25 Schelling, T.C., "Experimental Games and Bargaining Theory", in Knorr and Verba (1961), 47-68.

B26 Schelling, T.C., "What is Game Theory?", in Charlesworth (1967), 212-238.

B27 Shubik, M., "Game Theory and the Study of Social Behavior: An Introductory Exposition", in Shubik (1964), 3-77.

B28 Shubik, M., "The Uses of Game Theory", in Charlesworth (1967), 239-272.

B29 Slagle, J.R., "Artificial Intelligence and International Relations", in Bobrow and Schwartz (1968), 246-252.

B30 Smoker, P., "International Relations Simulations: A Summary", in Alker, Deutsch and Stoetzel (1973), 417-464.

B31 Snyder, R.C., "Some Perspectives on the Use of Experimental Techniques in the Study of International Relations", in Guetzkow (1963), 1-23.

B32 Solomon, L.N., "Simulation Research in International Decision-Making", in Sperrazzo (1965), 37-52.

B33 Waltz, K.N., "Realities, Assumptions and Simulations", in Coplin (1968), 105-111.

B34 Wohlstetter, A., "Sins and Games in America", in Shubik (1964), 209-225.

C - HISTORY OF INTERNATIONAL RELATIONS

C1 Adamthwaite, A., "[Franco-British] Reactions to the Munich Crisis", in Waites (1971), 170-199.

C2 Andrew, C., "The Entente Cordiale from its Origins to 1914", in Waites (1971), 11-39.

C3 Austen, R.A., "The Official Mind of Indirect Rule: British Policy in Tanganyika, 1916-1939", in Gifford and Louis (1967), 577-606.

C4 Austen, R.A., "Varieties of Trusteeship: African Territories under British and French Mandate, 1919-1939", in Gifford and Louis (1971), 515-541.

C5 Barraclough, G., "Europe and the Wider World in the Nineteenth and Twentieth Centuries", in Sarkissian (1961), 364-382.

C6 Baumont, M., "The Rhineland Crisis: 7 March 1936 [and Franco-British Relations]", in Waites (1971), 158-169.

C7 Bell, P.M.H., "The Breakdown of the [Franco-British] Alliance in 1940", in Waites (1971), 200-227.

C8 Beloff, M., "The Anglo-French Union Project of June 1940", in Mélanges Pierre Renouvin (1966), 199-219.

C9 Bemis, S.F., "The Shifting Strategy of American Defense and Diplomacy", in Lee and McReynolds (1949), 1-14.

C10 Benns, F.L., "The Two Paris Peace Conferences of the Twentieth Century", in Lee and McReynolds (1949), 153-170.

C11 Black, C.E., "Russian Interpretations of World History", in Rosenau, Davis and East (1972), 371-390.

C12 Blake, N.M., "England and the United States, 1897-1899", in Lee and McReynolds (1949), 257-283.

C13 Bley, H., "Social Discord in South West Africa, 1894-1904", in Gifford and Louis (1967), 607-630.

C14 Bloch, C., "Great Britain, German Rearmament, and the Naval Agreement of 1935", in Gatzke (1972), 125-151.

C15 Blum, J.M., "Limits of American Internationalism: 1941-45", in Krieger and Stern (1968), 387-401.

C16 Breuning, E., "Brockdorff-Rantzau: The 'Wanderer between Two Worlds'", in Abramsky (1974), 126-151.

C17 Brunschwig, H., "Anglophobia and French African Policy", in Gifford and Louis (1971), 3-34.

C18 Brunschwig, H., "Conclusion [Anglo-French rivalries in Africa in the nineteenth century]", in Gifford and Louis (1971), 397-406.

C19 Butler, J., "The German Factor in Anglo-Transvaal Relations", in Gifford and Louis (1967), 179-214.

C20 Carmoy, G. de., "Defence and Unity of Western Europe since 1958 [and Franco-British relations]", in Waites (1971), 344-374.

C21 Carroll, B.A., "The Historian and the [American] Dilemma of Power and Law in World Affairs ", in Barker (1971), 187-205.

C22 Chilver, E.M., "Paramountcy and Protection in the Cameroons: The Bali and the Germans, 1889-1913", in Gifford and Louis (1967), 479-511.

C23 Cohen, W.B., "The French Colonial Service in French West Africa", in Gifford and Louis (1971), 491-513.

C24 Collins, R.O., "Origins of the Nile Struggle: Anglo-German Negotiations and the Mackinnon Agreement of 1890", in Gifford and Louis (1967), 119-152.

C25 Craig, G.A., "Political and Diplomatic History", in Gilbert and Graubard (1972), 356-371.

C26 Craig, G.A., "The Revolution in War and Diplomacy [as a result of World War I]", in Roth (1967), 7-24.

C27 Current, R.N., "Consequences of the Kellogg Pact", in Anderson (1959), 210-229.

C28 Davis, P.C., "The New Diplomacy: The 1955 Geneva Summit Meeting", in Hilsman and Good (1965), 159-190.

C29 DeConde, A., "On Twentieth-Century Isolationism", in DeConde (1957), 3-32.

C30 Deschamps, H., "French Colonial Policy in Tropical Africa Between the Two World Wars", in Gifford and Louis (1971), 543-569.

C31 Duroselle, J.-B., "Strategic and Economic Relations [between Britain and France] during the First World War", in Waites (1971), 40-66.

C32 Fage, J.D., "British and German Colonial Rule: A Synthesis and Summary", in Gifford and Louis (1967), 691-706.

C33 Fieldhouse, D.K., "The Economic Exploitation of Africa: Some British and French Comparisons", in Gifford and Louis (1971), 593-662.

C34 Fifield, R.H., "The United States -- Paramount Power in the Pacific", in Lee and McReynolds (1949), 15-35.

C35 Fischer, F., "World Policy, World Power and German War Aims", in Koch (1972), 79-144.

C36 Freeman-Grenville, G.S.P., "Some Aspects of the External Relations of the East African Coast: Before 1800", in Ingham (1974), 69-83.

C37 Furet, F., "Quantitative History", in Gilbert and Graubard (1972), 45-61.

C38 Ganiage, J., "France, England, and the Tunisian Affair", in Gifford and Louis (1971), 35-72.

C39 Gardinier, D.E., "The British in the Cameroons, 1919-1939", in Gifford and Louis (1967), 513-555.

C40 Gardinier, D.E., "French Colonial Rule in Africa: A Bibliographical Essay", in Gifford and Louis (1971), 787-950.

C41 Garthoff, R.L., "The Cold War and the Changing Communist World", in Hilsman and Good (1965), 3-16.

C42 Gifford, P., "Indirect Rule: Touchstone or Tombstone for Colonial Policy?", in Gifford and Louis (1967), 351-391.

C43 Gifford, P., and Weiskel, T.C., "African Education in a Colonial Context: French and British Styles", in Gifford and Louis (1971), 663-711.

C44 Gilbert, F., "Intellectual History: Its Aims and Methods", in Gilbert and Graubard (1972), 141-158.

C45 Gillard, D.R., "Salisbury and the Indian Defence Problem, 1885-1902", in Bourne and Watt (1967), 236-248.

C46 Gordon, D.C., "Algeria, 1962-1967: An Essay on Dependence in Independence", in Gifford and Louis (1971), 749-776.

C47   Guillen, P., "The Entente of 1904 as a Colonial Settlement", in Gifford and Louis (1971), 333-368.

C48   Hall, H.D., "The British Commonwealth and the Founding of the League Mandate System", in Bourne and Watt (1967), 345-368.

C49   Halperin, S.W., "Italy and the Genesis of the League of Neutrals of August 1870", in *Mélanges Pierre Renouvin* (1966), 147-157.

C50   Hargreaves, J.D., "British and French Imperialism in West Africa, 1885-1898", in Gifford and Louis (1971), 261-283.

C51   Hess, R.L., "Germany and the Anglo-Italian Colonial Entente", in Gifford and Louis (1967), 153-178.

C52   Heussler, R., "British Rule in Africa", in Gifford and Louis (1971), 571-592.

C53   Hinsley, F.H., "Reflections on the History of International Relations", in Gilbert (1966), 19-34.

C54   Holborn, H., "Russia and the European Political System", in Lederer (1962), 377-415.

C55   Iliffe, J., "The Effects of the Maji Maji Rebellion of 1905-1906 on German Occupation Policy in East Africa", in Gifford and Louis (1967), 557-575.

C56   Ingham, K., "Foreign Relations of the Kingdoms of Western Uganda", in Ingham (1974), 161-187.

C57   Janssen, K.-H., "Gerhard Ritter: A Patriotic Historian's Justification [of his interpretation of the origins of the First World War]", in Koch (1972), 257-285.

C58   Johnson, D., "The Locarno Treaties [and Franco-British relations]", in Waites (1971), 100-124.

C59   Jonas, M., "The United States and the Failure of Collective Security in the 1930s", in Braeman, Bremner and Brody (1971), 241-293.

C60   Kanya-Forstner, A.S., "Military Expansion in the Western Sudan - French and British Style", in Gifford and Louis (1971), 409-441.

C61   Kaspi, A., "French War Aims in Africa, 1914-1919", in Gifford and Louis (1971), 369-396.

C62 Kelly, J.B., "Salisbury, Curzon and the Kuwait Agreement of 1899", in Bourne and Watt (1967), 249-290.

C63 Knoll, A.J., "Taxation in the Gold Coast Colony and in Togo: A Study in Early Administration", in Gifford and Louis (1967), 417-453.

C64 Koch, H.W., "Social Darwinism as a Factor in the 'New Imperialism'", in Koch (1972), 329-354.

C65 Kurat, Y.T., "How Turkey drifted into World War I", in Bourne and Watt (1967), 291-315.

C66 LaFeber, W., "American Foreign Policy in the Early Cold War: The Dilemmas of Historical Continuity", in Barker (1971), 37-54.

C67 Latourette, K.S., "The Spread of Christianity: British and German Missions in Africa", in Gifford and Louis (1967), 393-416.

C68 Lilienthal, A.M., "The Balfour Declaration: Forty Years Later", in Anderson (1959), 99-126.

C69 Loewenheim, F.L., "A Legacy of Hope and a Legacy of Doubt: Reflections on the Role of History and Historians in American Foreign Policy Since the Eighteenth Century", in Loewenheim (1967), 1-71.

C70 Louis, W.R., "The Berlin Congo Conference", in Gifford and Louis (1971), 167-220.

C71 Louis, W.R., "Great Britain and German Expansion in Africa, 1884-1919", in Gifford and Louis (1967), 3-46.

C72 Macartney, C.A., "Hungary's Declaration of War on the U.S.S.R. in 1941", in Sarkissian (1961), 153-165.

C73 Mackintosh, M., "Implications of the Sino-Soviet Dispute", in Erickson, Crowley and Galay (1966), 258-269.

C74 Manuel, F.E., "The Use and Abuse of Psychology in History", in Gilbert and Graubard (1972), 211-237.

C75 Marshall, D.B., "Free France in Africa: Gaullism and Colonialism", in Gifford and Louis (1971), 713-748.

C76 Mayer, A.J., "Domestic Causes of the First World War", in Krieger and Stern (1968), 286-300.

C77 Mayer, A.J., "Historical Thought and American Foreign Policy in the Era of the First World War", in Loewenheim (1967), 73-90.

C78 Mayer, S.L., "Anglo-German Rivalry at the Algeciras Conference", in Gifford and Louis (1967), 215-244.

C79 Medlicott, W.N., "The Coming of War in 1939", in Medlicott (1963), 231-256.

C80 Merritt, R.L., "Perspectives on History in Divided Germany", in Small (1970), 139-174.

C81 Miers, S., "The Brussels Conference of 1889-1890: The Place of the Slave Trade in the Policies of Great Britain and Germany", in Gifford and Louis (1967), 83-118.

C82 Miller, J.A., "The United States and Chinese Territorial Integrity, 1908", in Lee and McReynolds (1949), 233-256.

C83 Milward, A.S., "German Economic Policy Towards France, 1942-1944", in Bourne and Watt (1967), 423-443.

C84 Morton, L., "The Cold War and American Scholarship", in Loewenheim (1967), 123-169.

C85 Nevakivi, J., "Lord Kitchener and the Partition of the Ottoman Empire, 1915-1916", in Bourne and Watt (1967), 316-329.

C86 Newbury, C., "Partition, Development, Trusteeship: Colonial Secretary Wilheim Solf's West African Journey, 1913", in Gifford and Louis (1967), 455-477.

C87 Newbury, C., "The Tariff Factor in Anglo-French West African Partition", in Gifford and Louis (1971), 221-259.

C88 Nish, C., "Canada and the American Dilemma: Realism versus Idealism, 1945-1964", in Barker (1971), 66-81.

C89 Nish, I.H., "Japan and the Ending of the Anglo-Japanese Alliance", in Bourne and Watt (1967), 369-384.

C90 Obichere, B.I., "The African Factor in the Establishment of French Authority in West Africa, 1880-1900", in Gifford and Louis (1971), 443-490.

C91 Ørvik, N., "Nordic Security, Great Britain and the League of Nations", in Bourne and Watt (1967), 385-401.

C92 Paret, P., "The History of War", in Gilbert and Graubard (1972), 372-392.

C93 Pender-Cudlip, P., "The Iramba and Their Neighbours", in Ingham (1974), 55-66.

C94 Penson, Dame L.M., "Obligations by Treaty: Their Place in British Foreign Policy, 1898-1914", in Sarkissian (1961), 76-89.

C95 Pogue, F.C., "The Supreme Allied Command in Northern Europe, 1944-1945", in Lee and McReynolds (1949), 171-192.

C96 Proebst, H., "German-British Relations Since the War: A German View", in Kaiser and Morgan (1971), 191-202.

C97 Ramazani, R.K., "Treaty Relations: An Iranian-Soviet Case Study", in Lepawsky, Buehrig and Lasswell (1971), 298-311.

C98 Ramm, A., "Great Britain and France in Egypt, 1876-1882", in Gifford and Louis (1971), 73-119.

C99 Rotberg, R.I., "Resistance and Rebellion in British Nyasaland and German East Africa, 1888-1915: A Tentative Comparison", in Gifford and Louis (1967), 667-690.

C100 Rothfels, H., "The German Resistance [to Hitler] in its International Aspects", in Sarkissian (1961), 348-363.

C101 Russell, B., "Conciliating East and West", in Wright, Evan and Deutsch (1962), 263-272.

C102 Sainsbury, K., "The Second Wartime Alliance [between Britain and France]", in Waites (1971), 228-258.

C103 Sanderson, G.N., "The Origins and Significance of the Anglo-French Confrontation at Fashoda, 1898", in Gifford and Louis (1971), 285-331.

C104 Schlesinger, A., "The Historian as Participant", in Gilbert and Graubard (1972), 393-412.

C105 Schmitt, B.E., "The Origins of the First World War", in Medlicott (1963), 183-203.

C106 Schmokel, W.W., "The Hard Death of Imperialism: German and British Colonial Attitudes, 1919-1939", in Gifford and Louis (1967), 301-335.

C107 Schwarz, U., "Intervention: The Historical Development II", in Jaquet (1971), 29-39.

C108   Scott, W.E., "Neville Chamberlain and Munich: Two Aspects of Power", in Krieger and Stern (1968), 353-369.

C109   Sears, L.M., "Historical Revisionism Following the Two World Wars", in Anderson, (1959), 127-146.

C110   Shalloo, J.P., "United States Immigration Policy 1882-1948", in Lee and McReynolds (1949), 126-152.

C111   Siney, M.C., "The Allied Blockade Committee and the Inter-allied Trade Committees: the Machinery of Economic Warfare, 1917-1918", in Bourne and Watt (1967), 330-344.

C112   Smith, G., "The British Government and the Disposition of the German Colonies in Africa, 1914-1918", in Gifford and Louis (1967), 275-299.

C113   Stavrianos, L.S., "The United States and Greece: The Truman Doctrine in Historical Perspective", in Lee and McReynolds (1949), 36-59.

C114   Stengers, J., "British and German Imperial Rivalry: A Conclusion", in Gifford and Louis (1967), 337-347.

C115   Stengers, J., "King Leopold and Anglo-French Rivalry, 1882-1884", in Gifford and Louis (1971), 121-166.

C116   Stern, F., "Bethmann Hollweg and the War: The Limits of Responsibility", in Krieger and Stern (1968), 252-285.

C117   Strandmann, H.P. von, and Smith A., "The German Empire in Africa and British Perspectives: A Historiographical Essay", in Gifford and Louis (1967), 709-795.

C118   Swanson, M.W., "South West Africa in Trust, 1915-1939", in Gifford and Louis (1967), 631-665.

C119   Temperley, H.W.V., and Webster, C.K., "The Congress of Vienna 1814-15 and the Conference of Paris 1919", in Medlicott (1963), 1-24.

C120   Thimme, A., "Stresemann and Locarno", in Gatzke (1972), 73-93.

C121   Thomas, H., "[Britain and France:] Allies at Suez", in Waites (1971), 293-314.

C122   Thompson, L., "France and Britain in Africa: A Perspective", in Gifford and Louis (1971), 777-784.

C123 Toscano, M., "Eden's Mission to Rome on the Eve of the Italo-Ethiopian Conflict", in Sarkissian (1961), 126-152.

C124 Toynbee, A.J., "History by Teamwork", in Sarkissian (1961), 3-11.

C125 Turner, H.A., Jr., "Bismarck's Imperialist Venture: Anti-British in Origin?", in Gifford and Louis (1967), 47-82.

C126 Varg, P.A., "The United States as a World Power, 1900-1917: Myth or Reality?", in Braeman, Bremner and Brody (1971), 207-240.

C127 Waites, N., "The Depression Years [and Franco-British relations]", in Waites (1971), 125-157.

C128 Waller, B., "Bismarck and Gorchakov in 1879: 'The Two Chancellors' War'", in Bourne and Watt (1967), 209-235.

C129 Warner, G., "The Reconstruction and Defence of Western Europe after 1945 [and Franco-British relations]", in Waites (1971), 259-292.

C130 Waskow, A.I., "Peace and War: The History of the United States, 1939-1999", in Barker (1971), 168-184.

C131 Watson, D.R., "The Making of the Treaty of Versailles [and Franco-British relations]", in Waites (1971), 67-99.

C132 Watt, D.C.,"Anglo-German Relations Today and Tomorrow", in Kaiser and Morgan (1971), 203-218.

C133 Watt, D. C., "Contemporary History and the Survey of International Affairs", in Morgan (1972), 103-135.

C134 Watt, D.C., "The Initiation of the Negotiations Leading to the Nazi-Soviet Pact: A Historical Problem", in Abramsky (1974), 152-170.

C135 Watt, D.C., "South African Attempts to Mediate Between Britain and Germany", in Bourne and Watt (1967), 402-422.

C136 Willequet, J., "Anglo-German Rivalry in Belgian and Portuguese Africa?", in Gifford and Louis (1967), 245-273.

C137 Williams, A., "Security and Settlement in the Mediterranean since 1914 [and Franco-British relations]", in Waites (1971), 315-343.

C138 Williams, B.J., "The Revolution of 1905 and Russian Foreign Policy", in Abramsky (1974), 102-125.

C139 Younger, K.G., "Intervention: The Historical Development I", in Jaquet (1971), 12-28.

C140 Zechlin, E., "Cabinet versus Economic Warfare in Germany: Policy and Strategy during the Early Months of the First World War", in Koch (1972), 145-256.

D - INTERNATIONAL SYSTEM, ALLIANCE, BALANCE OF POWER

D1   Akzin, B., "On Great Powers and Super Powers", in Beyme (1971), 610-626.

D2   Alexandrowicz, C.H., "The Partition of Africa by Treaty", in Ingham (1974), 129-155.

D3   Allott, A., "The Changing Legal Status of Boundaries in Africa: A Diachronic View", in Ingham (1974), 111-126.

D4   Anderson, M.S., "Eighteenth-Century Theories of the Balance of Power", in Hatton and Anderson (1970), 183-198.

D5   Barston, R.P., "The External Relations of Small States", in Schou and Brundtland (1971), 39-56.

D6   Bell, C., "The Adverse Partnership", in Holbraad (1971), 25-40.

D7   Bjøl, E., "The Small State in International Politics", in Schou and Brundtland (1971), 29-37.

D8   Boulding, K.E., "The Learning and Reality-Testing Process in the International System", in Farrell and Smith (1967), 1-15.

D9   Boulding, K.E., "Stability in International Systems: The Role of Disarmament and Development", in Gray (1969), 193-210.

D10 Brams, S.J., "The Structure of Influence Relationships in the International System", in Rosenau (1969), 583-599.

D11 Brody, R.A., and Benham, A.H., "Nuclear Weapons and Alliance Cohesion", in Pruitt and Snyder (1969), 165-175.

D12 Buchan, A., "The Decline of American Primacy", in Mélanges Raymond Aron (1971), 435-453.

D13 Buchan, A., "Problems of an Alliance Policy: An Essay in Hindsight", in Howard (1965), 293-310.

D14 Bull, H., "Society and Anarchy in International Relations", in Butterfield and Wight (1966), 35-50.

D15 Burhoe, R.W., "The World System and Human Values", in Laszlo (1973), 161-185.

D16 Burns, A.L., "The Problems of Alliances", in Knorr and Read (1962), 163-198.

D17 Burton, J.W., "The Relevance [to civil conflict] of Behavioral Theories of the International System", in Moore (1974), 92-110.

D18 Butterfield, H., "The Balance of Power", in Butterfield and Wight (1966), 132-148.

D19 Chi, H.S., "The Chinese Warlord System as an International System", in Kaplan (1968), 405-425.

D20 Cohen, B.C., "National-International Linkages: Superpolities", in Rosenau (1969), 125-146.

D21 Davis, K., "Social Changes Affecting International Relations", in Rosenau (1961), 130-140.

D22 Deutsch, K.W., "The Crisis of Peace and Power in the Atom Age", in Bryson, Finkelstein and MacIver (1947a), 608-657.

D23 Deutsch, K.W., "Power and Communication in International Society", in de Reuck and Knight (1966), 300-316.

D24 Deutsch, K.W., and Kaplan, M.A., "The Limits of International Coalitions", in Rosenau (1964), 170-184.

D25 Dinerstein, H.S., "The United States and the Soviet Union: Standoff or Confrontation?", in Erickson, Crowley and Galay (1966), 270-284.

D26 Duchêne, F., "The Political Aspects of Intervention in Present Day International Politics II", in Jaquet (1971), 89-98.

D27 Duncan, W.G.K., "The Balance of Power and the Preservation of Peace", in Wallace (1957), 235-252.

D28 East, M.A., "Status Discrepancy and Violence in the International System: An Empirical Analysis", in Rosenau, Davis and East (1972), 299-319.

D29 FitzGerald, C.P., "Chinese Reactions to Tendencies Towards Condominium", in Holbraad (1971), 74-89.

D30 Fox, W.T.R., "The Study of 'Relations' in International Relations", in Lepawsky, Buehrig and Lasswell (1971), 386-400.

D31 Franke, W., "The Italian City-State System as an International System", in Kaplan (1968), 426-458.

D32   Friedman, J.R., "Alliance in International Politics", in Friedman, Bladen and Rosen (1970), 3-32.

D33   Golden, J., "System, Process and Decision-Taking: A Developing Method", in Kaplan (1968), 54-82.

D34   Graymer, L., "The Search for Patterns and Trends [in international politics]", in Graymer (1971), 177-196.

D35   Haines, R.L., "The Balance-of-Power System in Europe", in Graymer (1971), 9-32.

D36   Haines, R.L., "A Century of [international] System Change", in Graymer (1971), 33-63.

D37   Hoffmann, S., "Regulating the New International System", in Kilson (1975), 171-199.

D38   Holbraad, C., "Condominium and Concert", in Holbraad (1971), 1-24.

D39   Holst, J.J., "Small Powers in a Nuclear World", in Schou and Brundtland (1971), 197-194.

D40   Holsti, O.R., and Sullivan, J.D., "National-International Linkages: France and China as Nonconforming Alliance Members", in Rosenau (1969a), 147-195.

D41   Hudson, G.F., "Collective Security and Military Alliances", in Butterfield and Wight (1966), 176-180.

D42   Kaiser, K., "The Political Aspects of Intervention in Present Day International Politics I", in Jaquet (1971), 76-87.

D43   Kaplan, M.A., "Bipolarity in a Revolutionary Age", in Kaplan (1962), 251-266.

D44   Kaplan, M.A., "The Systems Approach to International Politics", in Kaplan (1968), 382-404.

D45   Kaplan, M.A., "Systems Theory", in Charlesworth (1967), 150-163.

D46   Landheer, B., "Is the World System Moving in a Pluralistic Direction?", in Boasson and Nurock (1973), 45-53.

D47   Laszlo, E., "Uses and Misuses of World System Models", in Laszlo (1973), 1-17.

D48   McClelland, C.A., "On the Fourth Wave: Past and Future in the Study of International Systems", in Rosenau, Davis and East (1972), 15-37.

D49   McClintock, C.G., Hekhuis, D.J., Burns, A.L., and Tucker, R.C., "A Pragmatic Approach to International Stability", in Hekhuis, McClintock and Burns (1964), 3-26.

D50   McWhinney, E., "The Historical Balance Sheet of 'Peaceful Coexistence' and of the Soviet-Western (bipolar) Détente", in Boasson and Nurock (1973), 19-31.

D51   Mead, M., "Models and Systems Analysis as Metacommunication", in Laszlo (1973), 19-28.

D52   Miller, E.H., "Canada's Role in the Origin of NATO", in Grob (1967), 251-290.

D53   Modelski, G., "Agraria and Industria: Two Models of the International System", in Knorr and Verba (1961), 118-143.

D54   Morgan, R., "The Role of Medium Powers in World Politics: the Case of Britain", in Kaiser and Morgan (1971), 261-276.

D55   Morgenthau, H.J., "From Great Powers to Superpowers", in Porter (1972), 129-139.

D56   Osgood, R.E., "NATO: The Entangling Alliance", in Stoessinger and Westin (1964), 66-101.

D57   Penrose, E.F., "Britain's Place in the Changing Structure of International Relations", in Penrose, Lyon and Penrose (1970), 28-79.

D58   Quester, G.H., "The World Political System", in Greenstein and Polsby (1975), vol. 8, 199-246.

D59   Rapoport, A., "U.S.-U.S.S.R.: Prospects for a Détente", in Gilbert (1973), 115-139.

D60   Reinken, D.L., "Computer Explorations of the 'Balance of Power': A Project Report", in Kaplan (1968), 459-481.

D61   Reynolds, P.A., "The Balance of Power: New Wine in an Old Bottle", in Ridley (1975), 230-242.

D62   Reynolds, P.A., "Factors Affecting the Number of Units in an International System", in Rajan (1971), 94-107.

D63   Richardson, J.L., "Super Powers and Secondary Powers: Western Europe and Japan", in Holbraad (1971), 90-104.

D64   Riggs, F.W., "International Relations as a Prismatic System", in Knorr and Verba (1961), 144-181.

D65   Rosen, S., "A Model of War and Alliance", in Friedman, Bladen and Rosen (1970), 215-237.

D66   Russett, B.M., "A Macroscopic View of International Politics", in Rosenau, Davis and East (1972), 109-124.

D67   Schwarz, H.-P., "The Roles of the Federal Republic [of Germany] in the Community of States", in Kaiser and Morgan (1971), 219-259.

D68   Scott, W.E., "Balance of Power as a Perennial Factor: French Motives in the Franco-Soviet Pact", in Hilsman and Good (1965), 207-228.

D69   Singer, J.D., "The Global System and Its Subsystems: A Developmental View", in Rosenau (1969), 21-43.

D70   Spiro, H.J., "An Evaluation of Systems Theory", in Charlesworth (1967), 164-174.

D71   Stourzh, G., "Some Reflections on Permanent Neutrality", in Schou and Brundtland (1971), 93-98.

D72   Sullivan, J.D., "Cooperating to Conflict: Sources of Informal Alignments", in Russett (1972), 115-138.

D73   Sullivan, J.D., "International Alliances", in Haas (1974), 99-122.

D74   Tatu, M., "East-West Relations", in Kohnstamm and Wolfgang (1973), 167-194.

D75   Taylor, A.M., "Some Political Implications of the Forrester [world system] Model", in Laszlo (1973), 29-68.

D76   Waltz, K.N., "International Structure, National Force, and the Balance of World Power", in Farrell and Smith (1968), 31-47.

D77   Wight, M., "The Balance of Power", in Butterfield and Wight (1966), 149-175.

D78   Wight, M., "The Balance of Power and the International Order", in James (1973), 85-115.

D79   Wilson, A., "Systems Epistemology", in Laszlo (1973), 119-140.

D80 Young, O.R., "Systemic Bases of Intervention", in Moore (1974), 111-126.

E - ACTORS, SOVEREIGNTY, THE STATE

E1 Bell, J.B., "Contemporary Revolutionary Organizations", in Keohane and Nye (1972), 153-168.

E2 Bell, P.D., "The Ford Foundation as a Transnational Actor", in Keohane and Nye (1972), 115-128.

E3 Beloff, M., "The Political Crisis of the European Nation-State", in Ionescu (1974), 25-31.

E4 Burks, R.V., "The Communist Polities of Eastern Europe [and national-international linkages]", in Rosenau (1969a), 275-303.

E5 Deutsch, K.W., "Between Sovereignty and Integration: Conclusion", in Ionescu (1974), 181-187.

E6 Deutsch, K.W., "On the Concepts of Politics and Power", in Farrell and Smith (1968), 48-57.

E7 Dion, L., "Anti-Politics and Marginals [in state stability]", in Ionescu (1974), 32-45.

E8 Eek, H., "The Conception of Small States", in Schou and Brundtland (1971), 11-13.

E9 Ehrlich, S., "State and Nation", in Beyme (1971), 486-496.

E10 Field, J.A., "Transnationalism and the New Tribe", in Keohane and Nye (1972), 3-22.

E11 Goodwin, G.L., "The Erosion of External Sovereignty", in Ionescu (1974), 100-117.

E12 Gough, K., "The Crisis of the Nation-State", in Fisher (1964), 41-69.

E13 Hinsley, F.H., "The Concept of Sovereignty and the Relations Between States", in Farrell and Smith (1968), 58-68.

E14 Holt, R.T., and Turner, J.E., "Insular Polities [and national-international linkages]", in Rosenau (1969a), 199-236.

E15 James, A., "The Contemporary Relevance of National Sovereignty", in Leifer (1972), 16-34.

E16   Jensen, L., "Postwar Democratic Polities: National-International Linkages in the Defense Policy of the Defeated States", in Rosenau (1969a), 304-323.

E17   Kaiser, K., "Interdependence and Autonomy: Britain and the Federal Republic in their Multinational Environment", in Kaiser and Morgan (1971), 17-40.

E18   Kaiser, K., "Transnational Relations as a Threat to the Democratic Process", in Keohane and Nye (1972), 356-370.

E19   Knorr, K., "Transnational Phenomena and the Future of the Nation-State", in Lepawsky, Buehrig and Lasswell (1971), 401-415.

E20   Merritt, R.L., "[Territorial] Noncontiguity and Political Integration", in Rosenau (1969a), 237-272.

E21   Niebuhr, R., "Power and Ideology in National and International Affairs", in Fox (1959), 107-118.

E22   Nye, J.S., "Transnational and Transgovernmental Relations", in Goodwin and Linklater (1975), 36-53.

E23   Nye, J.S., and Keohane, R.O., "Transnational Relations and World Politics: A Conclusion", in Keohane and Nye (1972), 371-398.

E24   Oakeshott, M., "The Vocabulary of a Modern European State", in Ridley (1975), 197-219.

E25   Rosenau, J.N., "Introduction [to linkage politics]: Political Science in a Shrinking World", in Rosenau (1969a), 1-17.

E26   Rosenau, J.N., "Toward the Study of National-International Linkages", in Rosenau (1969a), 44-63.

E27   Schilpp, P.A., "National Sovereignty and International Anarchy", in Ginsberg (1969), 152-162.

E28   Schmitt, H.O., "The National Boundary in Politics and Economics", in Merritt (1972), 405-422.

E29   Skjelsbaek, K., "The Growth of International Nongovernmental Organization in the Twentieth Century", in Keohane and Nye (1972), 70-92.

E30   Spiro, H.J., "Interdependence: A Third Option between Sovereignty and Supranational Integration", in Ionescu (1974), 143-163.

E31 Stankiewicz, W.J., "In Defence of Sovereignty: A Critique and An Interpretation", in Stankiewicz (1969), 3-38.

E32 Stankiewicz, W.J., "The Validity of the Concept of Sovereignty", in Stankiewicz (1969), 291-298.

E33 Strassoldo, R., "Boundaries in Society", in Reigersman-van der Eerden and Zoon (1974), 10-16.

E34 Vallier, I., "The Roman Catholic Church: A Transnational Actor", in Keohane and Nye (1972), 129-152.

E35 Vital, D., "The Analysis of Small Power Politics", in Schou and Brundtland (1971), 15-27.

E36 Warwick, D.P., "Transnational Participation and International Peace", in Keohane and Nye (1972), 305-324.

E37 Wolfers, A., "The Actors in International Politics", in Fox (1959), 83-106.

E38 Young, O.R., "The Actors in World Politics", in Rosenau, Davis and East (1972), 125-144.

F - NATIONALISM, ETHNICITY, RACE

F1 Avineri, S., "Political and Social Aspects of Israeli and Arab Nationalism", in Kamenka (1973), 100-122.

F2 Ball, W.M., "Nationalism as a Cause of War", in Wallace (1957), 157-177.

F3 Barbu, Z., "Nationalism as a Source of Aggression", in de Reuck and Knight (1966), 184-197.

F4 Barzun, J., "Cultural Nationalsim and the Makings of Fame", in Earle (1950), 3-17.

F5 Bossenbrook, W.J., "German Nationalism and Fragmentation", in Bossenbrook (1965), 13-32.

F6 Coleman, J.S., "Tradition and Nationalism in Tropical Africa", in Kilson (1975), 3-36.

F7 Cross, M., "Black Nationalism and Anti-colonialism", in Benewick, Berki and Parekh (1973), 299-319.

F8 Deutsch, K.W., "Research Problems on Race in Intranational and International Relations", in Shepherd and LeMelle (1970), 123-152.

F9 Dicks, H.V., "Some Psychological Studies of the German National Character", in Pear (1950), 193-218.

F10 Dodge, B., "The Significance of Religion in Arab Nationalism", in Proctor (1965), 94-119.

F11 Earle, E.M., "H.G. Wells, British Patriot in Search of a World State", in Earle (1950), 79-121.

F12 French, S., and Gutman, A., "The Principle of National Self-determination", in Held, Morgenbesser and Nagle (1974), 138-153.

F13 Gerson, L.L., "Immigrant Groups and American Foreign Policy", in Anderson (1959), 171-192.

F14 Hinsley, F.H., "The Impact of Nationalism [on international politics 1919-1969]", in Porter (1972), 183-210.

F15 Kamenka, E., "Political Nationalism - the Evolution of the Idea", in Kamenka (1973), 2-20.

F16 Kelman, H.C., "Patterns of Personal Involvement in the National System: A Social-psychological Analysis of Political Legitimacy", in Rosenau (1969), 276-288.

F17 Kohn, H., "French Nationalism and Western Unity", in Bossenbrook (1965), 33-49.

F18 Langsam, W.C., "Nationalism and History in the Prussian Elementary Schools under William II", in Earle (1950), 241-260.

F19 Lincoln, C.E., "The Race Problem and International Relations", in Shepherd (1970), 39-59.

F20 Martin, F.X., "The Evolution of a Myth - the Easter Rising, Dublin 1916", in Kamenka (1973), 56-80.

F21 Mead, M., "The Importance of National Cultures [in international relations]", in Hoffmann (1968), 89-105.

F22 Mead, M., "The Study of National Character", in Lerner and Lasswell (1951), 70-85.

F23 Meyer, A.G., "The Problem of National Minorities in the USSR", in Bossenbrook (1965), 51-68.

F24 Moss, J.A., "The Civil-Rights Movement and American Foreign Policy", in Shepherd (1970), 79-99.

F25 Mosse, G.L., "Mass Politics and the Political Liturgy of Nationalism", in Kamenka (1973), 38-54.

F26 Nye, J.S., "Nationalism, Statesmen, and the Size of African States", in Kilson (1975), 158-168.

F27 Peardon, T.P., "Sir John Seeley, Pragmatic Historian in a Nationalistic Age", in Earle (1950), 285-302.

F28 Plamenatz, J., "Two Types of Nationalism", in Kamenka (1973), 22-36.

F29 Rose, P.I., "The Development of Race Studies", in Shepherd and LeMelle (1970), 23-60.

F30 Rosenau, J.N., "Race in International Politics: A Dialogue in Five Parts", in Shepherd and LeMelle (1970), 61-122.

F31 Rowe, D.N., "American Diplomacy and Asian Nationalism in the Twentieth Century", in Anderson (1959), 23-42.

F32 Schuman, F.L., "The Neuroses of the Nations", in Lepawsky, Buehrig and Lasswell (1971), 312-323.

F33 Seabury, P., "Racial Problems and American Foreign Policy", in Shepherd (1970), 60-78.

F34 Shanahan, W.O., "Friedrich Naumann: A German View of Power and Nationalism", in Earle (1950), 352-398.

F35 Shepherd, G.W., Jr., "The Study of Race in American Foreign Policy and International Relations", in Shepherd and LeMelle (1970), 1-22.

F36 Ulam, A.B., "Nationalism, Panslavism, Communism", in Lederer (1962), 39-67.

F37 Van Den Bergh, G.v.B., "Contemporary Nationalism in the Western World", in Hoffmann (1968), 76-109.

F38 Vandenbosch, A., "Nationalism in South Africa", in Bossenbrook (1965), 69-93.

F39 VanDeusen, G.G., "The Nationalism of Horace Greeley", in Earle (1950), 431-454.

F40 Waite, R.G.L., "Adolf Hitler's Anti-Semitism: A Study in History and Psychoanalysis", in Wolman (1973), 192-230.

F41 Wang, G., "Nationalism in Asia", in Kamenka (1973), 82-98.

F42 Williams, G.M., "Communism's Impact on African Nationalism", in Bossenbrook (1965), 95-108.

F43 Wuorinen, J.H., "Scandinavia and the Rise of Modern National Consciousness", in Earle (1950), 455-479.

G - FOREIGN POLICY, DECISION-MAKING, INTERNAL/EXTERNAL LINKAGES

G1 Abrams, P., "Social Structure, Social Change, and British Foreign Policy", in Kaiser and Morgan (1971), 127-150.

G2 Allison, G.T., and Halperin, M.H., "Bureaucratic Politics: A Paradigm and Some Policy Implications", in Tanter and Ullman (1972), 40-79.

G3 Almond, G.A., "National Politics and International Politics", in Lepawsky, Buehrig and Lasswell (1971), 283-297.

G4 Aspaturian, V.V., "The Challenge of Soviet Foreign Policy", in Kaplan (1962), 209-232.

G5 Aspaturian, V.V., "Internal Politics and Foreign Policy in the Soviet System", in Farrell (1966), 212-287.

G6 Aspaturian, V.V., "Soviet Foreign Policy", in Macridis (1972), 174-237.

G7 Aspaturian, V.V., "The Soviet Union and International Communism", in Macridis (1972), 238-288.

G8 Baring, A., "The Institutions of German Foreign Policy", in Kaiser and Morgan (1971), 151-170.

G9 Bell, C., "China: The Communists and the World", in Northedge (1974), 120-160.

G10 Besson, W., "The Conflict of Traditions: the Historical Basis of West German Foreign Policy", in Kaiser and Morgan (1971), 61-80.

G11 Birnbaum, N., "Great Britain [and the revolution in world politics]: The Reactive Revolt", in Kaplan (1962), 31-68.

G12 Bishop, D.G., "The Cabinet and Foreign Policy [in the management of Britain's external relations]", in Boardman and Groom (1973), 137-160.

G13 Black, C.E., "The Pattern of Russian Objectives", in Lederer (1962), 3-38.

G14 Blanksten, G.I., "Fidel Castro and Latin America", in Kaplan (1962), 113-136.

G15   Boardman, R., and Groom, A.J.R., "Introduction: The Study of Britain's External Relations", in Boardman and Groom (1973), 1-27.

G16   Brzezinski, Z., "Dysfunctional Totalitarianism", in Beyme (1971), 375-389.

G17   Butler, W.E., "Soviet Attitudes Toward Intervention", in Moore (1974), 380-398.

G18   Buzan, B., "Internal Restraints on the Use of Force", in Northedge (1974a), 166-193.

G19   Bychowski, G., "Joseph V. Stalin: Paranoia and the Dictatorship of the Proletariat", in Wolman (1973), 115-149.

G20   Byrnes, R.F., "Attitudes Toward the West [in Russian foreign policy]", in Lederer (1962), 109-141.

G21   Cohen, B.C., "Foreign Policy Makers and the Press", in Rosenau (1961), 220-228.

G22   Cohen, B.C., and Harris, S.A., "Foreign Policy", in Greenstein and Polsby (1975), vol. 6, 381-437.

G23   Dallin, A., "The Use of International Movements [in Russian foreign policy]", in Lederer (1962), 311-349.

G24   Dallin, A., "Domestic Factors Influencing Soviet Foreign Policy", in Confino and Shimon (1973), 31-58.

G25   Deutsch, K.W., "External Influences on the Internal Behavior of States", in Farrell (1966), 5-26.

G26   Deutsch, K.W., Schweigler, G.L., and Edinger, L.J., "Foreign Policy of the German Federal Republic", in Macridis (1972), 119-173.

G27   Donelan, M., "The Elements of United States Policy", in Northedge (1974), 42-75.

G28   Duroselle, J.-B., "Changes in French Foreign Policy Since 1945", in Hoffmann et al. (1963), 305-358.

G29   East, M.A., and Hermann, C.F., "Do Nation-Types Account for Foreign Policy Behavior?", in Rosenau (1974), 269-304.

G30   Epstein, L.D., "British Foreign Policy", in Macridis (1972), 34-75.

G31 Farrell, R.B., "Foreign Policies of Open and Closed Political Societies", in Farrell (1966), 167-208.

G32 Figgures, F., "The Treasury and [Britain's] External Relations", in Boardman and Groom (1973), 161-172.

G33 Fisher, R., "Defects in the Governmental Decision Process", in Fisher (1964), 248-253.

G34 Forest, P. de, "The Social Sciences in the Foreign Policy Subsystem of Congress", in Crawford and Biderman (1969), 135-150.

G35 Franck, T.M., and Weisband, E., "Dissemblement, Secrecy, and Executive Privilege in the Foreign Relations of Three Democracies: A Comparative Analysis", in Franck and Weisband (1974), 399-441.

G36 Frankel, J., "The Intellectual Framework of British Foreign Policy", in Kaiser and Morgan (1971), 81-103.

G37 Friedrich, C.J., "International Politics and Foreign Policy in Developed (Western) Systems", in Farrell (1966), 97-119.

G38 Frohlich, N., and Oppenheimer, J.A., "Entrepreneurial Politics and Foreign Policy", in Tanter and Ullman (1972), 151-178.

G39 Galtung, J., "Social Position, Party Identification and Foreign Policy Orientation: A Norwegian Case Study", in Rosenau (1967), 161-193.

G40 Gehlen, M.P., "Political Elites in the Soviet Union and China", in Graymer (1971), 103-130.

G41 Greene, F., "The Intelligence Arm [of foreign policy]: The Cuban Missile Crisis", in Hilsman and Good (1965), 127-140.

G42 Greer, S., "Urbanization, Parochialism, and Foreign Policy", in Rosenau (1967), 253-261.

G43 Grinspoon, L., "Interpersonal Constraints and the Decision-Maker", in Fisher (1964), 239-247.

G44 Gurr, T.R., "The Relevance of Theories of Internal Violence for the Control of Intervention", in Moore (1974), 70-91.

G45 Gurtov, M., "The Style of Politics and Foreign Policy in Communist China", in Kitagawa (1969), 139-162.

G46 Halpern, A.M., "Communist China's Demands on the World", in Kaplan (1962), 233-247.

G47 Harf, J.E., Hoovler, D.G., and James, T.E., "Systemic and External Attributes in Foreign Policy Analysis", in Rosenau (1974), 235-250.

G48 Harrod, J., "State Management of Private Foreign Policy [in Britain's external relations]", in Boardman and Groom (1973), 289-304.

G49 Hermann, C.F., "Policy Classification: A Key to the Comparative Study of Foreign Policy", in Rosenau, Davis and East (1972), 58-79.

G50 Hermann, C.F., "What is a Foreign Policy Event?", in Hanrieder (1971), 295-321.

G51 Hermann, M.G., "Leader Personality and Foreign Policy Behavior", in Rosenau (1974), 201-234.

G52 Hilsman, R., "Orchestrating the Instrumentalities [of foreign policy]: The Case of Southeast Asia", in Hilsman and Good (1965), 191-203.

G53 Hirsch, F.E., "Stresemann and Adenauer: Two Great Leaders of German Democracy in Times of Crisis", in Sarkissian (1961), 266-280.

G54 Hoffmann, S., "Protest in Modern France", in Kaplan (1962), 69-91.

G55 Holcombe, A.N., "The American Presidency in the Nuclear Age", in Lepawsky, Buehrig and Lasswell (1971), 324-336.

G56 Holloway, D., "Foreign and Defence Policy [of the Soviet Union since the fall of Khrushchev]", in Brown and Kaiser (1975), 49-76.

G57 Holsti, O.R., "Political Processes and Foreign Policy: Decision Making in Crisis and Noncrisis Situations", in Graymer (1971), 67-102.

G58 Jensen, L., "Foreign Policy Calculation", in Haas (1974), 77-97.

G59 Johnson, J.E., "Policy Implications and Applications of International Relations Research for Foreign Policy and Diplomacy", in Palmer (1970), 229-239.

G60   Kaiser, K., and Morgan, R., "Introduction: Society and Foreign Policy -- Implications for Theory and Practice", in Kaiser and Morgan (1971), 1-15.

G61   Kaplan, M.A., "United States Foreign Policy in a Revolutionary Age", in Kaplan (1962), 431-466.

G62   Keenleyside, H.L., "Canada's Department of External Affairs", in Lee and McReynolds (1949), 60-82.

G63   Kissinger, H.A., "Domestic Structure and Foreign Policy", in Hoffmann (1968), 164-190.

G64   Larner, C., "The Organisation and Structure of the Foreign and Commonwealth Office", in Boardman and Groom (1973), 31-73.

G65   Lasswell, H.D., "Conflict and Leadership: The Process of Decision and the Nature of Authority", in de Reuck and Knight (1966), 210-228.

G66   Leifer, M., "Patterns of Indonesian Foreign Policy", in Northedge (1974), 349-376.

G67   Loewenberg, P., "Theodore Herzl: A Psychoanalytic Study in Charismatic Political Leadership", in Wolman (1973), 150-191.

G68   Long, N.E., "Open and Closed Systems", in Farrell (1966), 155-166.

G69   Lowi, T.J., "Making Democracy Safe for the World: National Politics and Foreign Policy", in Rosenau (1967), 295-331.

G70   Lyon, P., "Sources of Indian Foreign Policy", in Northedge (1974), 320-348.

G71   Macridis, R.C., "French Foreign Policy", in Macridis (1972), 76-118.

G72   Mapp, R.K., "Internal Environmental Influences and Foreign Policy", in Graymer (1971), 131-171.

G73   Marshall, C.B., "The Making of Foreign Policy in the United States", in Buehrig (1966), 37-60.

G74   McGowan, P.J., "Adaptive Foreign Policy Behavior: An Empirical Approach", in Rosenau (1974), 45-54.

G75   McGowan, P.J., "Problems in the Construction of Positive Foreign Policy Theory", in Rosenau (1974), 25-44.

G76 McLellan, D.S., "The Role of Political Style: A Study of Dean Acheson", in Hilsman and Good (1965), 229-256.

G77 Meehan, E.J., "The Concept 'Foreign Policy'", in Hanrieder (1971), 265-294.

G78 Milbrath, L.W., "Interest Groups and Foreign Policy", in Rosenau (1967), 231-251.

G79 Miller, W.E., "Voting and Foreign Policy", in Rosenau (1967), 213-230.

G80 Mishler, E.G., "The Peace Movement and the Foreign Policy Process", in Fisher (1964), 257-265.

G81 Moore, D.W., "Governmental and Societal Influences on Foreign Policy in Open and Closed Nations", in Rosenau (1974), 171-200.

G82 Moore, D.W., "National Attributes and National Typologies: A Look at the Rosenau Genotypes", in Rosenau (1974), 251-268.

G83 Morgenthau, H.J., "Emergent Problems of United States Foreign Policy", in Deutsch and Hoffmann (1971), 67-79.

G84 Morgenthau, H.J., "The American Tradition in Foreign Policy: An Overview", in Macridis (1972), 389-413.

G85 Narr, W.-D., "Social Factors Affecting the Making of Foreign Policy", in Kaiser and Morgan (1971), 105-126.

G86 Neu, C.E., "The Changing Interpretive Structure of American Foreign Policy", in Braeman, Bremner and Brody (1971), 1-57.

G87 Nielsen, K., "Social Science and American Foreign Policy", in Held, Morgenbesser and Nagel (1974), 286-319.

G88 Nish, I., "The Reemergence of Japan", in Northedge (1974), 296-319.

G89 Nolutshungu, S.C., "The Impact of External Opposition on South African Politics", in Thompson and Butler (1975), 369-399.

G90 Northedge, F.S., "The Adjustment of British Policy", in Northedge (1974), 161-202.

G91 Northedge, F.S., "The Nature of Foreign Policy", in Northedge (1974), 11-41.

G92   O'Leary, M.K., "Policy Formulation and Planning [in the management of Britain's external relations]", in Boardman and Groom (1973), 117-133.

G93   O'Leary, M.K., "Foreign Policy and Bureaucratic Adaptation", in Rosenau (1974), 55-70.

G94   Park, R.L., "India's Foreign Policy", in Macridis (1972), 367-388.

G95   Passin, H., "The Stratigraphy of Protest in Japan", in Kaplan (1962), 92-110.

G96   Pendill, C.G., "'Bipartisanship' in Soviet Foreign Policy-Making", in Hoffmann and Fleron (1971), 61-75.

G97   Pickles, D., "France: Tradition and Change", in Northedge (1974), 203-236.

G98   Pipes, R.E., "Domestic Politics and Foreign Affairs [in Russian foreign policy]", in Lederer (1962), 145-169.

G99   Pipes, R.E., "Some Operational Principles of Soviet Foreign Policy", in Confino and Shimon (1973) 5-30.

G100 Plischke, E., "Konrad Adenauer: Legator of the West German Governmental System", in Grob (1967), 153-202.

G101 Potholm, C.P., "The Effects on South Africa of Change in Contiguous Territories", in Thompson and Butler (1975), 329-348.

G102 Powell, C.A., Andrus, D., Fowler, W.A., and Knight, K., "Determinants of Foreign Policy Behavior: A Causal Modeling Approach", in Rosenau (1974), 151-170.

G103 Ranger, R., "The Canadian Perspective [on world affairs]", in Northedge (1974), 269-295.

G104 Reveley, W.T., III, "Constitutional Aspects of United States Participation in Foreign Internal Conflicts", in Moore (1974), 152-189.

G105 Richards, P.G., "Parliament and the Parties [in the management of Britain's external relations]", in Boardman and Groom (1973), 245-261.

G106 Roberts, H.L., "Russia and America", in Lederer (1962), 577-593.

G107 Robinson, J.A., "The Social Scientist and Congress", in Fisher (1964), 266-271.

G108 Robinson, J.A., and Snyder, R.C., "Decision-Making in International Politics", in Kelman (1965), 433-463.

G109 Rosenau, J.N., "Adaptive Strategies for Research and Practice in Foreign Policy", in Riggs (1971), 218-245.

G110 Rosenau, J.N., "Comparing Foreign Policies: Why, What, How", in Rosenau (1974), 3-22.

G111 Rosenau, J.N., "The External Environment as a Variable in Foreign Policy Analysis", in Rosenau, Davis and East (1972), 145-165.

G112 Rosenau, J.N., "Foreign Intervention as Adaptive Behavior", in Moore (1974), 129-151.

G113 Rosenau, J.N., "Foreign Policy as an Issue Area", in Rosenau (1967), 11-50.

G114 Rosenau, J.N., "Preferences and Political Responsibilities: The Relative Potency of Individual and Role Variables in the Behavior of U.S. Senators", in Singer (1968), 17-50.

G115 Rosenau, J.N., "The Premises and Promises of Decision-Making Analysis", in Charlesworth (1967), 189-211.

G116 Rosenau, J.N., "Pre-theories and Theories of Foreign Policy", in Farrell (1966), 27-91.

G117 Rosenau, J.N., and Hoggard, G.D., "Foreign Policy Behavior in Dyadic Relationships: Testing a Pre-Theoretical Extension", in Rosenau (1974), 117-150.

G118 Rostow, W.W., "The Planning of Foreign Policy", in Johnson (1964), 41-55.

G119 Rubinstein, A.Z., "Assessing Influence as a Problem in Foreign Policy Analysis", in Rubinstein (1975), 1-22.

G120 Rummel, R.J., "U.S. Foreign Relations: Conflict, Cooperation, and Attribute Distances", in Russett (1972), 71-113.

G121 Salmore, S.A., and Munton, D., "An Empirically Based Typology of Foreign Policy Behaviors", in Rosenau (1974), 329-352.

G122 Sampson, A., "The Institutions of British Foreign Policy", in Kaiser and Morgan (1971), 171-189.

G123   Sapin, B.M., "The Politico-Military Approach to American Foreign Policy", in Rosenau, Davis and East (1972), 320-344.

G124   Scalapino, R.A., "The Foreign Policy of Modern Japan", in Macridis (1972), 321-366.

G125   Schiebel, J., "The USSR in World Affairs: New Tactics, New Strategy", in Eissenstat (1975), 71-92.

G126   Scott, J., "The Convergence of Social Systems [and international relations]", in Hoffmann (1968), 188-197.

G127   Shaw, T.M., "African States and International Stratification: The Adaptive Foreign Policy of Tanzania", in Ingham (1974), 213-233.

G128   Stern, G., "Soviet Foreign Policy in Theory and Practice", in Northedge (1974), 76-119.

G129   Tandon, Y., "An Analysis of the Foreign Policy of African States: A Case Study of Uganda", in Ingham (1974), 191-209.

G130   Thompson, K.W., and Macridis, R.C., "The Comparative Study of Foreign Policy", in Macridis (1972), 1-33.

G131   Thorson, S.J., "National Political Adaptation", in Rosenau (1974), 71-114.

G132   Trask, D.F., "Writings on American Foreign Relations: 1957 to the Present", in Braeman, Bremner and Brody (1971), 58-118.

G133   Tucker, R.C., "Autocrats and Oligarchs [in Russian foreign policy]", in Lederer (1962), 171-195.

G134   Vatikiotis, P.J., "Islam and the Foreign Policy of Egypt", in Proctor (1965), 120-157.

G135   Velvel, L.R., "Selected Constitutional Issues Arising from Undeclared Wars", in Moore (1974), 190-214.

G136   Verba, S., "Assumptions of Rationality and Non-Rationality in Models of the International System", in Knorr and Verba (1961), 93-117.

G137   Wallace, W., "The Role of Interest Groups [in the management of Britain's external relations]", in Boardman and Groom (1973), 263-287.

G138   Waltz, K.N., "Electoral Punishment and Foreign Policy Crisis", in Rosenau (1967), 263-293.

G139   Whiting, A.S., "Foreign Policy of Communist China", in Macridis (1972), 289-320.

G140   Whiting, A.S., "The Scholar and the Policy-Maker", in Tanter and Ullman (1972), 229-247.

G141   Wilcox, W., "Forecasting Models and Foreign Policy", in Hanrieder (1971), 385-402.

G142   Windsor, P., "West Germany in Divided Europe", in Northedge (1974), 237-268.

G143   Yahuda, M.B., "Chinese Foreign Policy: A Process of Interaction", in Wilson (1973), 41-61.

G144   Zartman, I.W., "National Interest and Ideology [in African diplomacy]", in McKay (1966), 25-54.

G145   Zinnes, D.A., "Some Evidence Relevant to the Man-Milieu Hypothesis", in Rosenau, Davis and East (1972), 209-251.

H - INTERNATIONAL CONFLICT AND CRISIS

H1 Alger, C.F., "Decision-making Theory and Human Conflict", in McNeil (1965), 274-292.

H2 Angell, R.C., "The Sociology of Human Conflict", in McNeil (1965), 91-115.

H3 Beaumont, R.A., "Polemology: Promises and a Problem", in Beaumont and Edmonds (1975), 203-210.

H4 Black, C.E., "Conflict Management and World Order", in Black and Falk (1971), 3-14.

H5 Boulding, K.E., "Conflict Management as a Learning Process", in de Reuck and Knight (1966), 236-248.

H6 Boulding, K.E., "The Economics of Human Conflict", in McNeil (1965), 172-191.

H7 Brogan, D.W., "Conflicts Arising Out of Differing Governmental and Political Institutions", in Brookings Institution (1956), 37-64.

H8 Bronfenbrenner, U., "Allowing for Soviet Perceptions", in Fisher (1964), 161-178.

H9 Burton, J.W., "Conflict as a Function of Change", in de Reuck and Knight (1966), 370-401.

H10 Burton, J.W., "Conflicts of Interest: Subjective or Objective?", in Boasson and Nurock (1973), 253-259.

H11 Burton, J.W., "Functionalism and the Resolution of Conflict", in Groom and Taylor (1975), 238-249.

H12 Choucri, N., and North, R.C., "Dynamics of International Conflict: Some Policy Implications of Population, Resources, and Technology", in Tanter and Ullman (1972), 80-122.

H13 Deutsch, K.W., "Problems of Justice in International Territorial Disputes", in Bryson, Finkelstein and MacIver (1947), 237-270.

H14 Deutsch, M., "Producing Change in an Adversary", in Fisher (1964), 145-160.

H15 Deutsch, M., "A Psychological Approach to International Conflict", in Sperrazzo (1965), 1-19.

H16 East, M.A., "Status Discrepancy and Violence in the International System: An Empirical Analysis", in Rosenau, Davis and East (1972), 299-319.

H17 Epstein, F.T., "Germany and the United States: Basic Patterns of Conflict and Understanding", in Anderson (1959), 284-314.

H18 Falk, R.A., "World Law and Human Conflict", in McNeil (1965), 227-249.

H19 Fisher, R., "Fractionating Conflict", in Fisher (1964), 91-109.

H20 Gamson, W.A., "Evaluating Beliefs about International Conflict", in Fisher (1964), 27-40.

H21 Guelke, A., "Force, Intervention and Internal Conflict", in Northedge (1974a), 99-123.

H22 Haas, M., "International Conflict Resolution", in Haas (1974), 325-350.

H23 Haas, M., "International Socialization", in Haas (1974), 51-75.

H24 Haas, M., "Social Change and National Aggressiveness: 1900-1960", in Singer (1968), 215-244.

H25 Haas, M., "Sources of International Conflict", in Rosenau, Davis and East (1972), 252-277.

H26 Habicht, M., "Conflict Resolution by Peaceful Means", in Mudd (1967), 98-103.

H27 Harf, J.E., "Inter-Nation Conflict Resolution and National Attributes", in Rosenau (1974), 305-325.

H28 Hermann, C.F., "International Crisis as a Situational Variable", in Rosenau (1969), 409-421.

H29 Hermann, C.F., "Some Issues in the Study of International Crisis", in Hermann (1972), 3-17.

H30 Hermann, C.F., "Threat, Time, and Surprise: A Simulation of International Crisis", in Hermann (1972), 187-211.

H31 Hermann, C.F., and Brady, L.P., "Alternative Models of International Crisis Behavior", in Hermann (1972), 281-303.

H32 Hoffmann, S., "Perceptions, Reality, and the Franco-American Conflict", in Farrell and Smith (1967), 57-71.

H33 Holloway, R.L., "Human Aggression: The Need for a Species-Specific Framework", in Fried, Harris and Murphy (1967), 29-48.

H34 Holsti, O.R., "Time, Alternatives, and Communications: The 1914 and Cuban Missile Crises", in Hermann (1972), 58-80.

H35 Holsti, O.R., and North, R.C., "The History of Human Conflict", in McNeil (1965), 155-171.

H36 Holsti, O.R., North, R.C., and Brody, R.A., "Perception and Action in the 1914 Crisis", in Singer (1968), 123-158.

H37 Joynt, C.B., "John Foster Dulles and the Suez Crisis", in Grob (1967), 203-250.

H38 Katz, D., "Nationalism and Strategies of International Conflict Resolution", in Kelman (1965), 354-390.

H39 Kelman, H.C., "The Problem-Solving Workshop in Conflict Resolution", in Merritt (1972), 168-204.

H40 Kriesberg, L., "International Decisionmaking", in Haas (1974), 229-250.

H41 Lapter, K., "External and Internal Sources of International Tension", in de Reuck and Knight (1966), 351-369.

H42 Lentner, H.H., "The Concept of Crisis as Viewed by the United States Department of State", in Hermann (1972), 112-135.

H43 Lieberman, E.J., "Threat and Assurance in the Conduct of Conflict", in Fisher (1964), 110-122.

H44 Luard, E., "Civil Conflicts in Modern International Relations", in Luard (1972), 7-25.

H45 McClelland, C.A., "Access to Berlin: The Quantity and Variety of Events, 1948-1963", in Singer (1968), 159-186.

H46 McClelland, C.A., "The Acute International Crisis", in Knorr and Verba (1961), 182-204.

H47 McClelland, C.A., "The Beginning, Duration and Abatement of International Crises: Comparisons in Two Conflict Arenas", in Hermann (1972), 83-105.

H48 McClelland, C.A., "Systems Theory and Human Conflict", in McNeil (1965), 250-273.

H49 McClelland, C.A., and Hoggard, G.D.,"Conflict Patterns in the Interaction Among Nations", in Rosenau (1969), 711-724.

H50 McKay, V., "International Conflict Patterns [in African diplomacy]", in McKay (1966), 1-23.

H51 McNeil, E.B., "The Future of Human Conflict", in McNeil (1965), 309-315.

H52 McNeil, E.B., "The Nature of Aggression", in McNeil (1965), 14-41.

H53 McNeil, E.B., "The Nature of Social Science and Human Conflict", in McNeil (1965), 3-13.

H54 Mead, M., and Metraux, R., "The Anthropology of Human Conflict", in McNeil (1965), 116-138.

H55 Meyer, A.G., "An Anti-Anti-Communist Looks at Détente", in Eissenstat (1975), 323-332.

H56 Milburn, T.W., "The Management of Crisis", in Hermann (1972), 259-277.

H57 Milstein, J.S., "American and Soviet Influence, Balance of Power, and Arab-Israeli Violence", in Russett (1972), 139-166.

H58 North, R.C., "Perception and Action in the 1914 Crisis", in Farrell and Smith (1967), 103-122.

H59 Oeser, O.A., "Culture Patterns and Social Tensions", in Wallace (1957), 137-156.

H60 Paige, G.D., "Comparative Case Analysis of Crisis Decisions: Korea and Cuba", in Hermann (1972), 41-55.

H61 Rapoport, A., "Game Theory and Human Conflict", in McNeil (1965), 195-226.

H62 Rapoport, A., "Models of Conflict: Cataclysmic and Strategic", in de Reuck and Knight (1966), 259-287.

H63 Rapoport, A., "Rules for Debate [in East-West relations]", Wright, Evan and Deutsch (1962), 246-262.

H64 Rapoport, A., "Two Views on Conflict: The Cataclysmic and the Strategic Models", in International Peace Research Association (1966), 78-99.

H65 Reisman, W.M., "Sanctions and Enforcement [in the moderation of international conflict]", in Black and Falk (1971), 273-335.

H66   Richardson, L.F., "Threats and Security", in Pear (1950), 219-235.

H67   Roberts, A., "The Use of Civil Resistance in International Relations", in Wiener and Fisher, (1974), 113-133.

H68   Robinson, J.A., "Crisis: An Appraisal of Concepts and Theories", in Hermann (1972), 20-35.

H69   Robinson, J.A., Hermann, C.F., and Hermann, M.G., "Search Under Crisis in Political Gaming and Simulation", in Pruitt and Snyder (1969), 80-94.

H70   Rummel, R.J., "Dimensions of Foreign and Domestic Conflict Behavior: A Review of Empirical Findings", in Pruitt and Snyder (1969), 219-228.

H71   Rummel, R.J., "The Relationship Between National Attributes and Foreign Conflict Behavior", in Singer (1968), 187-214.

H72   Schwartz, D.C., "Decision Making in Historical and Simulated Crises", in Hermann (1972), 167-184.

H73   Singer, J.D., "The Political Science of Human Conflict", in McNeil (1965), 139-154.

H74   Sisson, R.L., and Ackoff, R.L., "Towards a Theory of the Dynamics of Conflict", in Mudd (1967), 125-142.

H75   Snyder, G.H., "Crisis Bargaining", in Hermann (1972), 217-256.

H76   Stagner, R., "The Psychology of Human Conflict", in McNeil (1965), 45-63.

H77   Stokes, W.S., "Cultural Anti-Americanism in Latin America", in Anderson (1959), 315-338.

H78   Sullivan, H.S., "Tension Interpersonal and International: A Psychiatrist's View", in Cantril (1950), 79-138.

H79   Sullivan, M.P., and Thomas, W., "Symbolic Involvement as a Correlate of Escalation: The Vietnam Case", in Russett (1972), 185-212.

H80   Tanter, R., "International System and Foreign Policy Approaches: Implications for Conflict Modelling and Management", in Tanter and Ullman (1972), 7-39.

H81 Tung, W.L., "Settlement of Disputes Through Nonamicable Means", in Lepawsky, Buehrig and Lasswell (1971), 97-119.

H82 Waltz, K.N., "Conflict in World Politics", in Speigel and Waltz (1971), 454-474.

H83 Waskow, A.I., "Nonlethal Equivalents of War", in Fisher (1964), 123-141.

H84 White, R.K., "Misperception of Aggression in Vietnam", in Farrell and Smith (1967), 123-140.

H85 Wilkes, D., "Territorial Stability and Conflict", in Black and Falk (1971), 165-209.

H86 Withey, S., and Katz, D., "The Social Psychology of Human Conflict", in McNeil (1965), 64-90.

H87 Wolfe, B.D., "Some Problems of the Russo-American Détente", in Eissenstat (1975), 333-344.

H88 Wright, Q., "The Social Sciences and International Conflict", in Rajan (1971), 67-82.

H89 Zinnes, D.A., "The Expression and Perception of Hostility in Prewar Crisis: 1914", in Singer (1968), 85-119.

H90 Zinnes, D.A., and Wilkenfeld, J., "An Analysis of Foreign Conflict Behavior of Nations", in Hanrieder (1971), 167-213.

H91 Zinnes, D.A., North, R.C., and Koch, H.E., Jr., "Capability, Threat, and the Outbreak of War", in Rosenau (1961), 469-482.

H92 Zinnes, D.A., Zinnes, J.L., and McClure, R.D., "Hostility in Diplomatic Communication: A Study of the 1914 Crisis", in Hermann (1972), 139-162.

J - NON-STRATEGIC DIMENSIONS OF WAR

J1 Alland, A., "War and Disease: An Anthropological Perspective", in Fried, Harris and Murphy (1967), 65-75.

J2 Allport, G.W., "The Role of Expectancy [as a cause of war]", in Cantril (1950), 43-78.

J3 Bedau, H.A., "Genocide in Vietnam?", in Held, Morgenbesser and Nagel (1974), 5-46.

J4 Bell, J.B., "Revolutionary Organisations [and international terrorism]: Special Cases and Imperfect Models", in Carlton and Schaerf (1975a), 78-92.

J5 Bennett, J.C., "Moral Urgencies in the Nuclear Context", in Bennett (1962), 93-121.

J6 Brodie, B., "Theories on the Causes of War", in *Mélanges Raymond Aron* (1971), vol. II, 367-384.

J7 Carpenter, C.R., "The Contribution of Primate Studies to the Understanding of War", in Fried, Harris and Murphy (1967), 49-58.

J8 Claude, I.L., "The Problem of Evaluating War", in Goodwin and Linklater (1975), 109-126.

J9 Cohen, M., "Morality and the Laws of War", in Held, Morgenbesser and Nagel (1974), 71-88.

J10 Coleman. D.C. , "War Demand and Industrial Supply: The 'Dope Scandal', 1915-1919", in Winter (1975), 205-227.

J11 Crawford, R.M., "Historical Aspects of the Problem of Recurrent Wars", in Wallace (1957), 3-21.

J12 Deane, P., "War and Industrialisation", in Winter (1975), 91-102.

J13 Decornoy, J., "Vietnam: The Real Issues", in Penrose, Lyon and Penrose (1970), 80-106.

J14 Deutsch, K.W., and Senghaas, D., "A Framework for a Theory of War and Peace", in Lepawsky, Buehrig and Lasswell (1971), 23-46.

J15 Diamond, S., "War and the Dissociated Personality", in Fried, Harris and Murphy (1967), 183-188.

J16 Dougherty, J.E., "The Political Context [of morality and modern warfare]", in Nagle (1960), 13-33.

J17 Dowty, A., "A Comparative Approach to the Study of International Conflict", in Carlton and Schaerf (1975), 193-201.

J18 Dunham, B., "The Categorical Imperative and the Cold War", in Ginsberg (1969), 187-197.

J19 Dunn, D., "War and Social Change", in Northedge (1974a), 220-247.

J20 Earle, E.M., "Hitler: The Nazi Concept of War", in Earle (1941), 504-516.

J21 Edmonds, M., "The Horizons of War: Problems of Projection", in Beaumont and Edmonds (1975), 1-20.

J22 Edmonds, M., "Reserve Forces: Mobilization Demands in Modern War", in Beaumont and Edmonds (1975), 35-54.

J23 Elkin, A.P., "War and the Biological Struggle for Existence", in Wallace (1957), 22-39.

J24 Eysenck, H.J., "War and Aggressiveness: A Survey of Social Attitude Studies", in Pear (1950), 49-81.

J25 Falk, R.A., "Ecocide, Genocide, and the Nuremburg Tradition of Individual Responsibility", in Held, Morgenbesser and Nagel (1974), 123-137.

J26 Friedrich, C.J., "War as a Problem of Government", in Ginsberg (1969), 163-184.

J27 Frondizi, R., "The Ideological Origins of the Third World War", in Ginsberg (1969), 77-95.

J28 Fuss, P., "The Problem-Solvers and the Public: Some Thoughts on Ellsberg, The Pentagon Papers, and the Degeneration of the American Polity", in French (1974), 85-97.

J29 Genova, A.C., "Can War be Rationally Justified?", in Ginsberg (1969), 198-221.

J30 Gewirth, A., "Reason and Conscience: The Claims of the Selective Conscientious Objector", in Held, Morgenbesser and Nagel (1974), 89-117.

J31 Glass, H.B., "The Biology of Nuclear War", in Barker (1963), 28-60.

J32   Grinspoon, L., "The Truth is Not Enough", in Fisher
        (1964), 272-281.

J33   Harris, J., "Social Planning in War-time: Some Aspects
        of the Beveridge Report", in Winter (1975), 239-256.

J34   Hartman, R.S., "The Revolution Against War", in Ginsberg
        (1969), 310-343.

J35   Harva, U., "War and Human Nature", in Ginsberg (1969),
        45-55.

J36   Hatfield, M.O., "Vietnam and American Values", in Lefever
        (1972), 74-94.

J37   Heradsveit, D., "The Role of International Terrorism in
        the Middle East Conflict and its Implications for
        Conflict Resolution", in Carlton and Schaerf (1975a),
        93-103.

J38   Herriott, R.M., "Biological Warfare", in Barker (1963),
        69-82.

J39   Horkheimer, M., "The Lessons of Fascism", in Cantril
        (1950), 209-242.

J40   Howard, M., "War as an Instrument of Policy", in
        Butterfield and Wight (1966), 193-200.

J41   Inglis, D.R., "The Nature of Nuclear War", in Bennett
        (1962), 41-66.

J42   Inglis, D.R., "Nuclear Warfare", in Barker (1963), 12-27.

J43   Janowitz, M., "The Emergent Military", in Beaumont and
        Edmonds (1975), 21-34.

J44   Jenkins, B.M., "International Terrorism: A New Mode of
        Conflict", in Carlton and Schaerf (1975a), 13-49.

J45   Kaplan, M.A., "Intervention in Internal War: Some Sys-
        tematic Sources", in Rosenau (1964), 92-121.

J46   Kerr, M., "Personality and Attitudes Towards Warfare",
        in Pear (1950), 83-90.

J47   Kronenberg, P.S., "Militia in the Seventies: A Conflict
        Paradigm", in Beaumont and Edmonds (1975), 110-134.

J48   Lang, B., "Papers from the Pentagon and the Matter of
        Individual and Corporate Responsibility", in French
        (1974), 110-134.

J49 Lasagna, L., "Chemical Warfare", in Barker (1963), 61-68.

J50 Lee, J., "Administrators and Agriculture: Aspects of German Agricultural Policy in the First World War", in Winter (1975), 229-238.

J51 Lesser, A., "War and the State", in Fried, Harris and Murphy (1967), 92-96.

J52 Livingstone, F.B., "The Effects of Warfare on the Biology of the Human Species", in Fried, Harris and Murphy (1967), 3-15.

J53 MacLeod, R. and K., "War and Economic Development: Government and the Optical Industry in Britain, 1914-18", in Winter (1975), 165-203.

J54 Margolis, J., "War and Ideology", in Held, Morgenbesser and Nagel (1974), 246-265.

J55 Matloff, M., "The American Approach to War", in Howard (1965), 213-243.

J56 Mead, M., "Alternatives to War", in Fried, Harris and Murphy (1967), 215-228.

J57 Mello, L.M.B. de, "The Biology of War and the Law of Peace", in Ginsberg (1969), 225-242.

J58 Melman, S., "Decision Making on War and Peace", in Fried, Harris and Murphy (1967), 229-234.

J59 Merton, T., "War and the Crisis of Language", in Ginsberg (1969), 99-119.

J60 Milstein, J.S., "The Vietnam War from the 1968 Tet Offensive to the 1970 Cambodian Invasion: A Quantitative Analysis", in Alker, Deutsch and Stoetzel (1973), 113-135.

J61 Modelski, G., "The International Relations of Internal War", in Rosenau (1964), 14-44.

J62 Modelski, G., "International Settlement of Internal War", in Rosenau (1964), 122-153.

J63 Murphy, G., "Political Invention As A Strategy Against War", in Sperrazzo (1965), 93-102.

J64 Naess, A., "The Function of Ideological Convictions [as a cause of war]", in Cantril (1950), 257-298.

J65 Nailor, P., "The Military Bureaucracy: A Case Study of a Civilian Contribution", in Beaumont and Edmonds (1975), 180-202.

J66 Nairn, R.C., "Counterguerrilla Warfare in Southeast Asia", in Kaplan (1962), 411-430.

J67 Nef, J., "Political, Technological and Cultural Aspects of War", in Ginsberg (1969), 120-137.

J68 Parsons, H.L., "Some Human Roots of Inhuman War", in Ginsberg (1969), 56-76.

J69 Paul, B.D., "The Direct and Indirect Biological Costs of War", in Fried, Harris and Murphy (1967), 76-80.

J70 Pear, T.H., "Peace, War and Culture Patterns", in Pear (1950), 21-45.

J71 Qadir, C.A., "God and War", in Ginsberg (1969), 260-283.

J72 Radway, L.I., "The Future of the Reserve Officer Training Corps", in Beaumont and Edmonds (1975) 56-68.

J73 Ramsey, P., "The Case for Making 'Just War' Possible", in Bennett (1962), 143-170.

J74 Reisman, M., "Private Armies in a Global War System: Prologue to Decision", in Moore (1974), 252-303.

J75 Richardson, L.F., "Statistics of Deadly Quarrels", in Pear (1950), 237-256.

J76 Rickman, J., "Psychodynamic Notes [on the causes of war]", in Cantril (1950), 167-208.

J77 Rosen, S., "War Power and the Willingness to Suffer", in Russett (1972), 167-183.

J78 Rosen, S., and Frank, R., "Measures Against International Terrorism", in Carlton and Schaerf (1975a), 60-68.

J79 Rosenau, J.N., "International Aspects of Internal War: A Working Paper", in Rosenau (1964), 289-311.

J80 Rosenau, J.N., "Internal War as an International Event", in Rosenau (1964), 45-91.

J81 Scott, A.M., "Internal Violence as an Instrument of Cold Warfare", in Rosenau (1964), 154-169.

J82 Service, E., "War and Our Contemporary Ancestors", in Fried, Harris and Murphy (1967), 160-167.

J83   Sharp, G., "The Social Structure and War", in Wallace (1957), 67-88.

J84   Shinn, R.L., "Faith and the Perilous [nuclear] Future", in Bennett (1962), 171-188.

J85   Singer, J.D., "Modern International War: From Conjecture to Explanation", in Lepawsky, Buehrig and Lasswell (1971), 47-71.

J86   Singer, J.D., Bremner, S., and Stuckey, J., "Capability Distribution, Uncertainty, and Major Power War, 1820-1965", in Russett (1972), 19-48.

J87   Singer, J.D., and Small, M., "Alliance Aggregation and the Onset of War, 1815-1945", in Singer (1968), 247-286.

J88   Sliwowski, G., "Legal Aspects of [international] Terrorism", in Carlton and Schaerf (1975a), 69-77.

J89   Somerville, J., "Marxism and War", in Ginsberg (1969), 138-151.

J90   Spits, Lt. Colonel Drs. F.C., "War and Revolution", in International Peace Research Association (1966), 99-116.

J91   Steinkraus, W.E., "War and the Philosopher's Duty", in Ginsberg (1969), 3-29.

J92   Szalai, A., "Social Tensions and Social Changes: A Marxist Analysis", in Cantril (1950), 23-41.

J93   Thieme, F.P., "The Biological Consequences of War", in Fried, Harris and Murphy (1967), 16-21.

J94   Toynbee, A.J., "War in Our Time", in Lepawsky, Buehrig and Lasswell (1971), 3-22.

J95   Trebilcock, C., "War and the Failure of Industrial Mobilisation: 1899 and 1914", in Winter (1975), 139-164.

J96   Vayda, A.P., "Hypotheses About Functions of War", in Fried, Harris and Murphy (1967), 85-91.

J97   Vigor, P.H., "The Soviet View of War", in MccGwire (1973), 16-30.

J98   Wallace, A.F.C., "Psychological Preparations for War", in Fried, Harris and Murphy (1967), 173-182.

J99   Wallace, M.D., "Status, Formal Organization, and Arms Levels as Factors Leading to the Onset of War, 1820-1964", in Russett (1972), 49-69.

J100 Wasserstrom, R., "The Responsibility of the Individual for War Crimes", in Held, Morgenbesser and Nagel (1974), 47-70.

J101 Wiles, P., "War and Economic Systems", in <u>Mélanges Raymond Aron</u> (1971), vol. II, 269-297.

J102 Williams, A., "Youthful Officer Retirement: Matrix for Political Action", in Beaumont and Edmonds (1975), 69-88.

J103 Zahn, G.C., "Social Science and the Theology of War", in Nagle (1960), 104-125.

J104 Zasloff, J.J., "Peasant Protest in South Viet Nam", in Kaplan (1962), 192-206.

K - STRATEGIC THOUGHT, DETERRENCE THEORY, DEFENCE POLICY

K1   Alexander, A.J., "Weapons Acquisition in the Soviet Union, the United States, and France", in Horton, Rogerson and Warner (1974), 426-444.

K2   Baynes, J.C.M., "British Military Ideology", in Horton, Rogerson and Warner (1974), 39-52.

K3   Beaton, L., "Capabilities of Non-Nuclear Powers", in Buchan (1966), 13-38.

K4   Benington, H.D., "Command and Control for Selective [military] Response", in Knorr and Read (1962), 117-141.

K5   Blaker, J.R., "Weapons Acquisition: China", in Horton, Rogerson and Warner (1974), 444-452.

K6   Booth, K., "Military Power, Military Force, and Soviet Foreign Policy", in MccGwire (1973), 31-56.

K7   Brinton, C., Craig, G.A., and Gilbert, F., "Jomini [as a maker of modern strategy]", in Earle (1941), 77-92.

K8   Brodie, B., "New Techniques of War and National Policies", in Ogburn (1949), 144-173.

K9   Brown, N., "The Evolution of British Strategic Thought", in Horton, Rogerson and Warner (1974), 233-244.

K10 Brown, N., "Towards a More Dangerous World?", in Twitchett (1971), 48-81.

K11 Burns, A.L., "The Nth Country Problem, Mutual Deterrence and International Stability", in Hekhuis, McClintock and Burns (1964), 114-133.

K12 Chang, P.H., "Mao Tse-tung and his Generals: Some Observations on Military Intervention in Chinese Politics", in Horton, Rogerson and Warner (1974), 121-128.

K13 Chapman, J.W., "Coercion in Politics and Strategy", in Pennock and Chapman (1972), 289-319.

K14 Cohen, S.P., "Military Ideology: South Asia", in Horton, Rogerson and Warner (1974), 73-87.

K15 Craig, G.A., "Delbrück: The Military Historian", in Earle (1941), 260-283.

K16   Crane, R.D., "Psychostrategy: A New Concept", in Erickson, Crowley and Galay (1966), 229-238.

K17   Davis, V., "The Office of the Secretary of Defense and the U.S. Department of Defense", in Rosenau, Davis and East (1972), 345-370.

K18   DeWeerd, H.A., "Churchill, Lloyd George, Clemenceau: The Emergence of the Civilian [in military history]", in Earle (1941), 287-305.

K19   Earle, E.M., "Adam Smith, Alexander Hamilton, Friedrich List: The Economic Foundations of Military Power", in Earle (1941), 117-154.

K20   Earle, E.M., "Lenin, Trotsky, Stalin: Soviet Concepts of War", in Earle (1941), 322-364.

K21   Erickson, J., "Introduction. Nuclear Strategy: World Dilemma", in Erickson, Crowley and Galay (1966), 1-19.

K22   Ficks, R.S., "The Burgeoning Arsenal: Developments and Projections", in Beaumont and Edmonds (1975), 135-156.

K23   Galay, N., "The Soviet Approach to the Modern Military Revolution", in Erickson, Crowley and Galay (1966), 20-34.

K24   Garder, M., "The Impact on Land Warfare [of nuclear power]", in Erickson, Crowley and Galay (1966), 142-147.

K25   Garthoff, R., "Military Power in Soviet Policy", in Erickson, Crowley and Galay (1966), 239-257.

K26   Garthoff, R., "Military Influences and Instruments [in Russian foreign policy]", in Lederer (1962), 243-277.

K27   Gibbs, N., "British Strategic Doctrine, 1918-1939", in Howard (1965), 185-212.

K28   Gibson, I.M., "Maginot and Liddell Hart: The Doctrine of Defense", in Earle (1941), 365-387.

K29   Gilbert, F., "Machiavelli: The Renaissance of the Art of War", in Earle (1941), 3-25.

K30   Glennon, J.P., "'This Time Germany is a Defeated Nation': The Doctrine of Unconditional Surrender and Some Unsuccessful Attempts to Alter It, 1943-44", in Grob (1967), 109-152.

K31   Gohlert, E.W., "An Organizational Perspective on German National Security Policy", in Horton, Rogerson and Warner (1974), 146-155.

K32   Gottmann, J., "Bugeaud, Galliéni, Lyauty: The Development of French Colonial Warfare", in Earle (1941), 234-259.

K33   Gray, C., "Strategic Ideas and Defence Policy: The Organizational Nexus", in Beaumont and Edmonds (1975), 89-109.

K34   Green, P., "Strategy, Politics, and Social Scientists", in Kaplan (1973), 39-68.

K35   Greenwood, D., "The Defense Efforts of France, West Germany, and the United Kingdom", in Horton, Rogerson and Warner (1974), 340-362.

K36   Gregory, F., and Simpson, J., "The Acquisition of Military Aircraft in Great Britain and West Germany", in Horton, Rogerson and Warner (1974), 453-464.

K37   Guerlac, H., "Vauban: The Impact of Science on War", in Earle (1941), 26-48.

K38   Hammond, P.Y., "The Cross-National Comparison of Force Postures", in Horton, Rogerson and Warner (1974), 298-309.

K39   Handel, M.I., "The Development of the Israeli Political-Military Doctrine", in Horton, Rogerson and Warner (1974), 279-289.

K40   Harding, H., "The Evolution of Chinese Military Policy", in Horton, Rogerson and Warner (1974), 216-232.

K41   Head, R.G., "The Weapons Acquisition Process: Alternative National Strategies", in Horton, Rogerson and Warner (1974), 412-425.

K42   Heinlein, J.J., "China's Force Posture: Factors in the Policy Process", in Horton, Rogerson and Warner (1974), 326-339.

K43   Herz, J.H., "International Politics and the Nuclear Dilemma", in Bennett (1962), 15-38.

K44   Holborn, H., "Moltke and Schlieffen: The Prussian-German School [of military thinking]", in Earle (1941), 172-205.

K45   Horelick, A.L., "Perspectives on the Study of Comparative Military Doctrine", in Horton, Rogerson and Warner (1974), 192-200.

K46   Howard, M., "Changes in the Use of Force, 1919-1969", in Porter (1972), 140-159.

K47   Howard, M., "Jomini and the Classical Tradition in Military Thought", in Howard (1965), 3-20.

K48   Howard, M., "Morality and Force in International Politics", in MacKinnon (1969), 75-91.

K49   Hudson, G.F., "Threats of Force in International Relations", in Butterfield and Wight (1966), 201-205.

K50   Hurewitz, J.C., "Weapons Acquisition: Israel and Egypt", in Horton, Rogerson and Warner (1974), 482-493.

K51   Kahn, H., "The Arms Race and World Order", in Kaplan (1962), 332-351.

K52   Kahn, H., "Some Comments on Controlled War", in Knorr and Read (1962), 32-66.

K53   Kahn H., "Strategy, Foreign Policy, and Thermonuclear War", in Goldwin (1963), 43-70.

K54   Kanter, A., and Thorson, S.J., "The Weapons Procurement Process: Choosing Among Competing Theories", in Rosen (1973), 157-196.

K55   Kaplan, M.A., "Limited Retaliation as a Bargaining Process", in Knorr and Read (1962), 142-162.

K56   Kaplan, M.A., "The Sociology of Strategic Thinking", in Lepawsky, Buehrig and Lasswell (1971), 85-96.

K57   Kavic. L.J., "Force Posture: India and Pakistan", in Horton, Rogerson and Warner (1974), 376-390.

K58   Kemp, G., "Israel and Egypt: Military Force Posture 1967-1972", in Horton, Rogerson and Warner (1974), 391-405.

K59   Kinney, K., "The Use of Force by the Great Powers", in Northedge (1974a), 36-69.

K60   Kiralfy, A., "Japanese Naval Strategy", in Earle (1941), 457-484.

K61   Kissinger, H.A., "American Strategic Doctrine and Diplomacy", in Howard (1965), 271-292.

K62 Knorr, K., "Limited Strategic War", in Knorr and Read (1962), 3-31.

K63 Knorr. K., "Notes on the Analysis of National Capabilities", in Rosenau, Davis and East (1972), 175-186.

K64 Kolodziej, E.A., "French Military Doctrine", in Horton, Rogerson and Warner (1974), 245-258.

K65 Korb, L.J., "The [United States] Secretary of Defense and the Joint Chiefs of Staff: The Budgetary Process", in Sarkesian (1972), 301-340.

K66 Lambeth, B.S., "The Sources of Soviet Military Doctrine", in Horton, Rogerson and Warner (1974), 200-216.

K67 Levine, E.P., "Methodological Problems in Research on the Military-Industrial Complex", in Rosen (1973), 291-307.

K68 Lieberson, S., "An Empirical Study of Military-Industrial Linkages", in Rosen (1973), 61-83.

K69 Luvaas, J., "European Military Thought and Doctrine, 1870-1914", in Howard (1965), 69-93.

K70 Mackintosh, J.M., "The Development of Soviet Military Doctrine Since 1918", in Howard (1965), 247-269.

K71 Mackintosh, J.M., "Soviet Military Policy", in MccGwire (1973), 57-69.

K72 McIntosh, D., "Coercion and International Politics: A Theoretical Analysis", in Pennock and Chapman (1972), 243-271.

K73 Melman, S., "Alternative Strategies and Budgets for Military Security", in Sarkesian (1972), 167-200.

K74 Miksche, F.O., "Is the Atomic Deterrent a Bluff?", in Erickson, Crowley and Galay (1966), 35-51.

K75 Milburn, T.W., "Intellectual History of a Research Program [Project Michelson] ", in Pruitt and Snyder (1969), 263-283.

K76 Millis, W., "The Uselessness of Military Power", in Goldwin (1963), 22-42.

K77 Moriarty, J.K., "Technology, Strategy and National Military Policy", in Nagle (1960), 34-57.

K78   Nailor, P., "Defence Policy and Foreign Policy [in the management of Britain's external relations]", in Boardman and Groom (1973), 221-241.

K79   Nailor, P., "The Problem of Security in Europe", in Twitchett (1971), 110-140.

K80   Naroll, R., "Deterrence in History", in Pruitt and Snyder (1969), 150-164.

K81   Neumann, S., "Engels and Marx: Military Concepts of the Social Revolutionaries", in Earle (1941), 155-171.

K82   Northedge, F.S., "The Resort to Arms", in Northedge (1974a), 11-35.

K83   Ørvik, N., "Scandinavian Military Doctrines", in Horton, Rogerson and Warner (1974), 258-272.

K84   Osgood, R.E., "The Uses of Military Power in the Cold War", in Goldwin (1963), 1-21.

K85   Palmer, R.R., "Frederick the Great, Guibert, Bülow: From Dynastic to National War", in Earle (1941), 49-74.

K86   Paret, P., "Clausewitz and the Nineteenth Century", in Howard (1965), 21-41.

K87   Peterson, P.A., "Soviet Perceptions of Military Sufficiency: 1960-74", in Eissenstat (1975), 249-266.

K88   Pool, I.d.S., "Deterrence as an Influence Process", in Pruitt and Snyder (1969), 189-196.

K89   Possony, S.T., and Mantoux, E., "Du Picq and Foch: The French School [of military thought]", in Earle (1941), 206-233.

K90   Quester, G.H., "Naval Arms Races: Functional or Symbolic?", in Quester (1975), 17-41.

K91   Rapoport, A., "Critique of Strategic Thinking", in Fisher (1964), 211-237.

K92   Raser, J.R., "International Deterrence", in Haas (1974), 301-324.

K93   Raser, J.R., and Crow, W.J., "A Simulation Study of Deterrence Theories", in International Peace Research Association (1966), 146-165.

K94   Read, T., "Limited Strategic War and Tactical Nuclear War", in Knorr and Read (1962), 67-116.

K95   Rees, D., "Towards the McNamara Doctrine", in Erickson, Crowley and Galay (1966), 80-92.

K96   Roherty, J.M., "Policy Implications and Applications of International Relations Research for Defense and Security", in Palmer (1970), 183-200.

K97   Ropp, T., "Continental Doctrines of Sea Power", in Earle (1941), 446-456.

K98   Rosen, S., "Testing the Theory of the Military-Industrial Complex", in Rosen (1973) 1-25.

K99   Rothfels, H., "Clausewitz [as a maker of modern strategy]", in Earle (1941), 93-113.

K100 Ruebensaal, J.D., "Substitutes for Force: The Example of Subversion", in Northedge (1974a), 124-145.

K101 Russett, B.M., "A Countercombatant Deterrent? Feasibility, Morality, and Arms Control", in Sarkesian (1972), 201-242.

K102 Schelling, T.C., "Comment [on limited strategic war]", in Knorr and Read (1962), 241-258.

K103 Slater, J., and Nardin, T., "The Concept of a Military-Industrial Complex", in Rosen (1973), 27-60.

K104 Smoke, R., "National Security Affairs", in Greenstein and Polsby (1975), vol. 8, 247-362.

K105 Speier, H., "Ludendorff: The German Concept of Total War", in Earle (1941), 306-321.

K106 Sprout, M.T., "Mahan: Evangelist of Sea Power", in Earle (1941), 415-445.

K107 Twitchett, K.J., "Strategies for Security: Some Theoretical Considerations", in Twitchett (1971), 1-47.

K108 Vinson, J.C., "Military Force and American Policy, 1919-1939", in DeConde (1957), 56-81.

K109 Warner, E., "Douhet, Mitchell, Seversky: Theories of Air Warfare", in Earle (1941), 485-503.

K110 Warner, E.L., "Soviet Strategic Force Posture: Some Alternative Explanations", in Horton, Rogerson and Warner (1974), 310-325.

K111 Weinstein, M.E., "Japan's Defense Policy and the Self-Defense Forces", in Horton, Rogerson and Warner (1974), 363-375.

K112 Whittlesey, D., "Haushofer: The Geopoliticians *sic* ", in Earle (1941), 388-411.

K113 Wilcox, W.A., "The Indian Defense Industry: Technology and Resources", in Horton, Rogerson and Warner (1974), 479-482.

K114 Wolfe, T.W., "Trends in Soviet Thinking on Theater Warfare and Limited War", in Erickson, Crowley and Galay (1966), 52-79.

K115 Wolfe, T.W., "Soviet Strategic Policy", in MccGwire (1973), 70-81.

K116 Wolfowitz, P.D., "The Pot and the Kettle, or Rationality Within Reason: Mr. Green's Deadly Logic", in Kaplan (1973), 69-100.

L - ARMS CONTROL, DISARMAMENT, NUCLEAR PROLIFERATION

L1 Bader, W.B., "The Proliferation of Conventional Weapons", in Black and Falk (1971), 210-223.

L2 Barker, C.A., "Disarmament: A Problem of Time", in Barker (1963), 1-11.

L3 Bayandor, D., "Maintenance of the NPT [Treaty on the Non-Proliferation of Nuclear Weapons] in the 1970s: The Asian Dimension", in Cordier (1971), 198-228.

L4 Bellany, I., "The Central Balance: Arms Race and Arms Control", in Holbraad (1971), 41-63.

L5 Bethill, C.D., "Nonmilitary Incentives for the Acquisition of Nuclear Weapons", in Cordier (1971), 40-64.

L6 Birnbaum, K., "The Swedish Experience [nuclear proliferation]", in Buchan (1966), 68-75.

L7 Blaker, J.R., "The Production of Conventional Weapons in Communist China ", in Whitson (1972), 215-227.

L8 Buchan, A., "Introduction [to nuclear proliferation]", in Buchan (1966), 1-11.

L9 Burns, A.L., "Problems of Disarmament", in Hekhuis, McClintock and Burns (1964), 189-207.

L10 Chalfont, Lord, "Alternatives to Proliferation: Inhibition by Agreement", in Buchan (1966), 123-142.

L11 Daiches, D., "Renouncing Nuclear Weapons", in Wright, Evan and Deutsch (1962), 206-212.

L12 Feiveson, H., "Arms Control and Disarmament", in Black and Falk (1971), 336-369.

L13 Frank, J.D., "Psychological Aspects of the Disarmament Problem", in Barker (1963), 82-97.

L14 Fromm, E., "The Case for Unilateral Disarmament", in Wright, Evan and Deutsch (1962), 178-191.

L15 Fromm, E., "Explorations into the Unilateral Disarmament Position", in Bennett (1962), 125-139.

L16 Galtung, J., "Public Opinion on the Economic Effects of Disarmament", in Benoit (1967), 171-180.

L17   Gupta, S., "The Indian Dilemma [nuclear proliferation]", in Buchan (1966), 55-67.

L18   Hammond, P.Y., "Nonmilitary Instruments of Policy in a Disarming and Disarmed World", in Wolfers et al. (1966), 55-87.

L19   Hoffmann, S., "Nuclear Proliferation and World Politics", in Buchan (1966), 89-121.

L20   Hopmann, P.T., "Internal and External Influences on Bargaining in Arms Control Negotiations: The Partial Test Ban", in Russett (1972), 213-237.

L21   Horner, C., "The Production of Nuclear Weapons in Communist China ", in Whitson (1972), 229-252.

L22   Howard, M., "Problems of a Disarmed World", in Butterfield and Wight (1966), 206-214.

L23   Inglis, D.R., "Transition to Disarmament", in Goldwin (1963), 92-111.

L24   Kramish, A., "The Proliferation of Nuclear Weapons", in Black and Falk (1971), 224-251.

L25   Lough, T.S., "Psychology, Psychologists and Disarmament", in Sperrazzo (1965), 80-92.

L26   Millar, T.B., "The Nuclear Non-Proliferation Treaty and Super Power Condominium", in Holbraad (1971), 64-73.

L27   Mills, E.S., "The Economic Effects of Arms Control", in Barker (1963), 143-157.

L28   Osgood, C.E., "Graduated Unilateral Initiatives for Peace", in Wright, Evan and Deutsch (1962), 161-177.

L29   Osgood, R.E., "Military Power in a Disarming and Disarmed World", in Wolfers et al.(1966), 33-53.

L30   Schwarz, U., "Inhibition Through Policy: The Role of the Non-Nuclear Powers", in Buchan (1966), 143-164.

L31   Sibley, M.Q., "Unilateral Disarmament", in Goldwin (1963), 112-140.

L32   Singer, J.D., "Disarmament: The Domestic and Global Context", in Gilbert (1973), 175-200.

L33   Smith, K.W., and Merritt, J.N., "Some Complexities of Arms Control Planning", in Sarkesian (1972), 245-274.

L34 Sommer, T., "The Objectives of Germany [nuclear proliferation]", in Buchan (1966), 39-54.

L35 Svala, G., "Sweden's View of the Non-Proliferation Treaty", in Cordier (1971), 94-115.

L36 Talensky, N., "Anti-Missile Systems and Disarmament", in Erickson, Crowley and Galay (1966), 219-228.

L37 Urban, L., "Some Effects of Disarmament on Research and Development", in Benoit (1967), 161-170.

L38 Wakaizumi, K., "The Problem for Japan [nuclear proliferation]", in Buchan (1966), 76-87.

L39 Wolfers, A., "Disarmament, Peacekeeping, and the National Interest", in Wolfers et al. (1966), 3-32.

L40 Yarmolinsky, A., "The [United States] President, the Congress, and Arms Control", in Sarkesian (1972), 277-299.

M - DIPLOMACY, BARGAINING, NEGOTIATION

M1   Bennett, E.M., "Joseph C. Grew: The Diplomacy of Pacification", in Burns and Bennett (1974), 65-90.

M2   Boahen, A.A., "Fante Diplomacy in the Eighteenth Century", in Ingham (1974), 25-49.

M3   Brown, S.D., "Shidehara Kijūrō: The Diplomacy of the Yen", in Burns and Bennett (1974), 201-226.

M4   Buckley, T., "John Van Antwerp MacMurray: The Diplomacy of an American Mandarin", in Burns and Bennett (1974), 27-48.

M5   Burns, R.D., "Stanley K. Hornbeck: The Diplomacy of the Open Door", in Burns and Bennett (1974), 92-117.

M6   Butler, R., "Paradiplomacy", in Sarkissian (1961), 12-25.

M7   Butterfield, Sir H., "Diplomacy", in Hatton and Anderson (1970), 357-372.

M8   Butterfield, H., "The New Diplomacy and Historical Diplomacy", in Butterfield and Wight (1966), 181-192.

M9   Cameron, E.R., "Alexis Saint-Léger Léger [and interwar diplomacy]", in Craig and Gilbert (1953), 378-405.

M10 Challener, R.D., "The French Foreign Office: The Era of Philippe Berthelot", in Craig and Gilbert (1953), 49-85.

M11 Chu, Pao-chin, "V.K. Wellington Koo: The Diplomacy of Nationalism", in Burns and Bennett (1974), 125-152.

M12 Conroy, H., "Nomura Kichisaburō: The Diplomacy of Drama and Desperation", in Burns and Bennett (1974), 297-316.

M13 Coox, A.D., "Shigemitsu Mamoru: The Diplomacy of Crisis", in Burns and Bennett (1974), 251-274.

M14 Coplin, W.D., "Recent Trends in the Social Sciences Related to Instruction in Diplomacy", in Simpson (1972), 139-151.

M15 Craig, G.A., "The British Foreign Office from Grey to Austen Chamberlain", in Craig and Gilbert (1953), 15-48.

M16 Craig, G.A., "The German Foreign Office from Neurath to Ribbentrop", in Craig and Gilbert (1953), 406-436.

M17 Craig, G.A., "Techniques of Negotiation [in Russian foreign policy]", in Lederer (1962), 351-373.

M18 Craig, G.A., "Totalitarian Approaches to Diplomatic Negotiation", in Sarkissian (1961), 107-125.

M19 Davison, R.H., "Turkish Diplomacy from Mudros to Lausanne", in Craig and Gilbert (1953), 172-209.

M20 Duroselle, J.B., "Changes in Diplomacy Since Versailles", in Porter (1972), 105-128.

M21 Eban, A., "Conflict Between Nations", in Mudd (1967), 84-86.

M22 Farnsworth, L., "Hirota Kōki: The Diplomacy of Expansionism", in Burns and Bennett (1974), 227-250.

M23 Ferrell, R.H., "Woodrow Wilson and Open Diplomacy", in Anderson (1959), 193-209.

M24 Flack, M.J., "The Objectives and Purposes of Instruction in Diplomacy", in Simpson (1972), 77-87.

M25 Ford, F.L., "Three Observers in Berlin:Rumbold, Dodd, and Francois-Ponçet", in Craig and Gilbert (1953), 437-476.

M26 Ford, F.L., and Schorske, C.E., "The Voice in the Wilderness: Robert Coulondre [and interwar diplomacy]", in Craig and Gilbert (1953), 555-578.

M27 Gilbert, F., "Ciano and his Ambassadors", in Craig and Gilbert (1953), 512-536.

M28 Gilbert, F., "Two British Ambassadors: Perth and Henderson", in Craig and Gilbert (1953), 537-554.

M29 Hambro, E., "Some Notes on Parliamentary Diplomacy", in Friedmann, Henkin and Lissitzyn (1972), 280-297.

M30 Heston, E.L., "Papal Diplomacy: Its Organization and Way of Acting", in Gurian and Fitzsimons (1954), 33-47.

M31 Hodgkin, T., "Diplomacy and the Diplomats in the Western Sudan", in Ingham (1974), 3-22.

M32 Holborn, H., "Diplomats and Diplomacy in the Early Weimar Republic", in Craig and Gilbert (1953), 123-171.

M33   Hughes, H.S., "The Diplomacy of Italian Fascism, 1922-1932", in Craig and Gilbert (1953), 210-233.

M34   Huizenga, J., "Yosuke Matsuoka and the Japanese-German Alliance", in Craig and Gilbert (1953), 615-648.

M35   Hyer, P., "Hu Shih: The Diplomacy of Gentle Persuasion", in Burns and Bennett (1974), 153-170.

M36   Ikle, F.C., "Bargaining and Communication", in Pool, Schramm, et al. (1973), 836-843.

M37   Jervis, R., "Bargaining and Bargaining Tactics", in Pennock and Chapman (1972), 272-288.

M38   Kaufmann, W.W., "Two American Ambassadors: Bullitt and Kennedy", in Craig and Gilbert (1953), 649-681.

M39   Kemp, A., "Summit Conferences during World War II as Instruments of American Diplomacy", in Anderson (1959), 256-283.

M40   Kirk-Greene, A.H.M., "Diplomacy and Diplomats: The Formation of Foreign Service Cadres in Black Africa", in Ingham (1974), 279-319.

M41   Kissinger, H.A., "Reflections on Power and Diplomacy", in Johnson (1964), 17-39.

M42   Laue, T.H. von, "Soviet Diplomacy: G.V. Chicherin, Peoples Commissar for Foreign Affairs, 1918-1930", in Craig and Gilbert (1953), 234-281.

M43   Levi, W., "International Statecraft", in Haas (1974), 151-175.

M44   Lin, Han-sheng, "Chou Fo-hai: The Diplomacy of Survival", in Burns and Bennett (1974), 171-193.

M45   Lonnroth, E., "The Diplomacy of Östen Undén", in Craig and Gilbert (1953), 86-99.

M46   Nobel, J.W., "Competition and Co-operation in International Politics as a Bargaining Problem", in International Peace Research Association (1966), 116-140.

M47   Oppenheim, A.N., and Smart, I., "The British Diplomat", in Boardman and Groom (1973), 75-116.

M48   Plischke, E., "The Optimum Scope of Instruction in Diplomacy", in Simpson (1972), 1-25.

M49　Poullada, L.B., "Appraisal of Resources and Problems of Instruction in Diplomacy", in Simpson (1972), 219-234.

M50　Roberts, H.L., "The Diplomacy of Colonel Beck", in Craig and Gilbert (1953), 579-614.

M51　Roberts, H.L., "Maxim Litvinov [and interwar diplomacy]", in Craig and Gilbert (1953), 344-377.

M52　Rosecrance, R.N., "Diplomacy in Security Systems", in Gray (1969), 93-107.

M53　Ross, G., "W. Cameron Forbes: The Diplomacy of a Darwinist", in Burns and Bennett (1974), 49-64.

M54　Sawyer, J., and Guetzkow, H., "Bargaining and Negotiation in International Relations", in Kelman (1965), 464-520.

M55　Schorske, C.E., "Two German Ambassadors: Dirksen and Schulenburg", in Craig and Gilbert (1953), 477-511.

M56　Simpson, S., "Liberal Arts Instruction in Diplomacy", in Simpson (1972), 272-289.

M57　Teters, B., "Matsuoka Yōsuke: The Diplomacy of Bluff and Gesture", in Burns and Bennett (1974), 275-296.

M58　Timberlake, C.E., "The Summit Meeting as a Form of Diplomacy in American-Soviet Relations in the 1970s", in Eissenstat (1975), 93-118.

M59　Wadsworth, J.J., "Atoms for Peace", in Stoessinger and Westin (1964), 33-65.

M60　Walker, R.L., "The Developing Role of Cultural Diplomacy in Asia", in Anderson (1959), 43-62.

M61　Winkler, H.R., "Arthur Henderson [and interwar diplomacy]", in Craig and Gilbert (1953), 311-343.

M62　Wood, H.J., "Nelson Trusler Johnson: The Diplomacy of Benevolent Pragmatism", in Burns and Bennett (1974), 7-26.

M63　Zinner, P.E., "Czechoslovakia: The Diplomacy of Eduard Benes", in Craig and Gilbert (1953), 100-122.

N - COMMUNICATION, PUBLIC OPINION, PROPAGANDA, PSYCHOLOGICAL ASPECTS OF INTERNATIONAL RELATIONS

N1 Abt, C.C., and Pool, I.d.S., "The Constraint of Public Attitudes [on strategic military decisions]", in Knorr and Read (1962), 199-240.

N2 Alger, C.F., "Personal Contact in Intergovernmental Organizations", in Kelman (1965), 521-547.

N3 Angell, R.C., "International Communication and the World Society", in Wright (1948), 145-160.

N4 Barghoorn, F.C., "Propaganda: Tsarist and Soviet [in Russian foreign policy]", in Lederer (1962), 279-309.

N5 Bobrow, D.B., "Transfer of Meaning Across National Boundaries", in Merritt (1972), 33-61.

N6 Clapp, P.A., and Halperin, M.H., "U.S. Elite Images of Japan: The Postwar Period", in Iriye (1975), 202-222.

N7 Cohen, B.C., "Mass Communication and Foreign Policy", in Rosenau (1967), 195-212.

N8 Cohen, B.C., "The Relationship Between Public Opinion and the Foreign Policy Maker", in Small (1970), 65-80.

N9 Cook, W.G., "Propaganda and War", in Wallace (1957), 193-213.

N10 Coser, L., "The Role of Groups [in international relations]: Contributions of Sociology", in Hoffman (1968), 106-123.

N11 Davison, W.P., "International and World Public Opinion", in Pool, Schramm, et al. (1973), 871-886.

N12 Deutsch, K.W., "Communication Models and Decision Systems", in Charlesworth (1967), 273-299.

N13 Deutsch, K.W., "Communication Theory and Political Integration", in Jacob and Toscano (1964), 46-74.

N14 Deutsch, K.W., "The Impact of Communications upon International Relations Theory", in Said (1968), 74-92.

N15 Deutsch, K.W., "Self-Referent Symbols and Self-Referent Communication Patterns: A Note on Some Pessimistic Theories of Politics", in Bryson, Finkelstein, MacIver and McKeon (1954), 619-646.

N16   Deutsch, K.W., and Merritt, R.L., "Effects of Events on National and International Images", in Kelman (1965), 130-187.

N17   Deutsch, K.W., and Senghaas, D., "The Fragile Sanity of States: A Theoretical Analysis", in Kilson (1975), 200-244.

N18   Dicks, H.V., "The International Soldier - A Psychiatrist's View", in Bloomfield (1964), 236-256.

N19   Elliott, P., and Golding, P., "The [British] News Media and Foreign Affairs", in Boardman and Groom (1973), 305-330.

N20   Frankel, C., "Educational and Cultural Relations", in Hoffman (1968), 7-23.

N21   Free, L.A., "Public Opinion Research [and international relations]", in Hoffman (1968), 48-63.

N22   Free, L.A., "The Role of Public Opinion in International Relations", in Crawford and Biderman (1969), 214-222.

N23   Geiger, T., and Hansen, R.D., "The Role of Information and Decision Making on Foreign Aid", in Bauer and Gergen (1968), 329-380.

N24   Glazer, N., "From Ruth Benedict to Herman Kahn: The Postwar Japanese Image in the American Mind", in Iriye (1975), 138-168.

N25   Iriye, A., "Japan as a Competitor, 1895-1917", in Iriye (1975), 73-99.

N26   Isaacs, H.R., "Sources for Images of Foreign Countries", in Small (1970), 91-105.

N27   Janis, I.L., and Smith, M.B., "Effects of Education and Persuasion on National and International Images", in Kelman (1965), 188-235.

N28   Janowitz, M., "Content Analysis and the Study of the 'Symbolic Environment'", in Rogow (1969), 155-170.

N29   Jervis, R., "Consistency in Foreign Policy Views", in Merritt (1972), 272-291.

N30   Kecskemeti, P., "Propaganda", in Pool, Schramm, et al. (1973), 844-870.

N31   Kirk, G., "Mass Aspirations and International Relations", in Brookings Institution (1956), 1-18.

N32   Kitagawa, J.M., "Introduction: Western Understanding of the East", in Kitagawa (1969), 21-41.

N33   Lasswell, H.D., "The Climate of International Action", in Kelman (1965), 337-353.

N34   Lerner, D., "Managing Communication for Modernization: A Developmental Construct", in Rogow (1969), 171-196.

N35   Lerner, D., "Psychology and Psychological Operations [in international relations]", in Hoffman (1968), 124-136.

N36   Lerner, D., "Strategy of Truth: Symbol and Act in World Propaganda", in Bryson, Finkelstein, MacIver and McKeon (1954), 371-382.

N37   Mancall, M., "Two Realities [Sino-American relations]", in Kitagawa (1969), 229-250.

N38   Manning, R., "International News Media", in Hoffman (1968), 147-167.

N39   Maynard, H., "The Language of International Communication: Semantics and Linguistics", in Hoffman (1968), 137-146.

N40   McClosky, H., "Personality and Attitude Correlates of Foreign Policy Orientation", in Rosenau (1967), 51-109.

N41   Merritt, R.L., "Transmission of Values Across National Boundaries", in Merritt (1972), 3-32.

N42   Merritt, R.L., "The USIA [United States Information Agency] Surveys: Tools for Policy and Analysis", in Merritt and Puchala (1968), 3-30.

N43   Mishler, A.L., "Personal Contact in International Exchanges", in Kelman (1965), 548-561.

N44   Miwa, K., "Japanese Images of a War with the United States", in Iriye (1975), 115-137.

N45   Norman, J., "Influence of Pro-Fascist Propaganda on American Neutrality, 1935-1936", in Lee and McReynolds (1949), 193-214.

N46   North, R.C., "The Analytical Prospects of Communications Theory", in Charlesworth (1967), 300-316.

N47   Perkins, D., "The Department of State and American Public Opinion", in Craig and Gilbert (1953), 282-308.

N48   Peterson, S., "Events, Mass Opinion, and Elite Attitudes", in Merritt (1972), 252-271.

N49 Phillips, W.R., "International Communications", in Haas (1974), 178-201.

N50 Pool, I.d.S., "Content Analysis and the Intelligence Function", in Rogow (1969), 197-223.

N51 Pool, I.d.S., "Effects of Cross-National Contact on National and International Images", in Kelman (1965), 104-129.

N52 Pool, I.d.S., "Public Opinion", in Pool, Schramm, et al. (1973), 779-835.

N53 Pruitt, D.G., "Definition of the Situation as a Determinant of International Action", in Kelman (1965), 391-432.

N54 Rapoport, A., "Perceiving the Cold War", in Fisher (1964), 13-26.

N55 Richman, A., "Public Opinion and Foreign Affairs: The Mediating Influence of Educational Level", in Merritt (1972), 232-251.

N56 Rosenberg, M.J., "Images in Relation to the Policy Process: American Public Opinion on Cold-War Issues", in Kelman (1965), 277-334.

N57 Rosenberg, M.J., "Attitude Change and Foreign Policy in the Cold War Era", in Rosenau (1967), 111-159.

N58 Russett, B.M., "The Revolt of the Masses: Public Opinion on Military Expenditures", in Russett (1972), 299-319.

N59 Russett, B.M., "Elite Perceptions and Theories of World Politics", in Goodwin and Linklater (1975), 86-108.

N60 Saeki, S., "Images of the United States as a Hypothetical Enemy", in Iriye (1975), 100-114.

N61 Sargeant, H.H., "Communications to Open and Closed Societies", in Hoffman (1968), 168-187.

N62 Saul, L.J., "Preventive Psychiatry and World Problems", in Mudd (1967), 34-38.

N63 Schiller, H.I., "Madison Avenue Imperialism", in Merritt (1972), 318-338.

N64 Schmitt, B.E., "The Relation of Public Opinion and Foreign Affairs Before and During the First World War", in Sarkissian (1961), 322-330.

N65 Scott, W.A., "Psychological and Social Correlates of International Images", in Kelman (1965), 70-103.

N66 Small, M., "Historians Look at Public Opinion", in Small (1970), 13-32.

N67 Speier, H., "Psychological Warfare Reconsidered", in Lerner and Lasswell (1951), 252-270.

N68 Stoessinger, J.G., "China and America: The Burden of Past Misperceptions", in Farrell and Smith (1967), 72-91.

N69 Tillman, S., "American Perceptions of China", in Kitagawa (1969), 251-270.

N70 Wabeke, B.H., "1790: A Turning Point in the Life of a Word [Propaganda]", in Reigersman-van der Eerden and Zoon (1974), 53-58.

N71 Wedge, B., "Communication Analysis and Comprehensive Diplomacy", in Hoffman (1968), 24-47.

N72 Welch, S., "The American Press and Indochina, 1950-56", in Merritt (1972), 207-231.

N73 White, R.K., "Images in the Context of International Conflict: Soviet Perceptions of the U.S. and the U.S.S.R.", in Kelman (1965), 236-276.

N74 Wright, Q., "Symbols of Nationalism and Internationalism", in Bryson, Finkelstein, MacIver and McKeon (1954), 383-403.

P - ETHICS, MORALITY, IDEAS, VALUES, IDEOLOGY

P1 Aron, R., "Political Action in the Shadow of Atomic Apocalypse", in Lasswell and Cleveland (1962), 445-457.

P2 Baier, K., "[My Lai:] Guilt and Responsibility", in French (1972), 35-61.

P3 Bates, S., "My Lai and Vietnam: The Issues of Responsibility", in French (1972), 145-165.

P4 Bouthoul, G., "Definitions of Terror", in Carlton and Schaerf (1975a), 50-59.

P5 Bozeman, A.B., "Biography and the Thought-world of the West", in Reigersman-van der Eerden and Zoon (1974), 1-4.

P6 Bull, H., "The Grotian Conception of International Society", in Butterfield and Wight (1966), 51-73.

P7 Burtt, E.A., "Philosophers as Warriors", in Ginsberg (1969), 30-42.

P8 Butterfield, H., "Morality and an International Order", in Porter (1972), 336-357.

P9 Carr, E.H., "The Moral Foundations for World Order", in Woodward, et al. (1949), 53-75.

P10 Cole, C.W., "The Heavy Hand of Hegel", in Earle (1950), 64-78.

P11 Cooper, D., "[My Lai:] Responsibility and the 'System'", in French (1972), 81-100.

P12 Couloumbis, T.A., "Traditional Concepts [of international relations] and the 'Greek Reality'", in Said (1968), 160-175.

P13 Cropsey, J., "The Moral Basis of International Action", in Goldwin (1963), 71-91.

P14 Current, R.N., "The United States and 'Collective Security': Notes on the History of an Idea", in DeConde (1957), 33-55.

P15 D'Amato, A., "The Relevance of Machiavelli to Contemporary World Politics", in Parel (1972), 209-224.

P16   Downie, R.S., "[My Lai:] Responsibility and Social Roles", in French (1972), 63-80.

P17   Dunn, D., "The Papal-Communist Détente, 1963-73: Its Evolution and Causes", in Eissenstat (1975), 121-140.

P18   Fain, H., "[My Lai:] Some Moral Infirmities of Justice", in French (1972), 17-34.

P19   French, P.A., "[My Lai:] The Responsibility of Monsters and Their Makers", in French (1972), 1-15.

P20   Gibb, H.A.R., "Religion and Politics in Christianity and Islam", in Proctor (1965), 3-23.

P21   Good, R.C., "National Interest and Moral Theory: The 'Debate' Among Contemporary Realists", in Hilsman and Good (1965), 271-292.

P22   Goodwin, G.L., "An International Morality?", in Parekh and Berki (1972), 99-113.

P23   Held, V., "[My Lai:] Moral Responsibility and Collective Action", in French (1972), 101-118.

P24   Jackson, R., "Divergent Philosophical Approaches to Foreign Policy", in Corbet and Jackson (1974), 48-59.

P25   Kaplan, M.A., "The Education of a Moral Primitive", in Kaplan (1973), 149-154.

P26   Kaplan, M.A., "Freedom in History and International Politics", in Rosenau, Davis and East (1972), 96-105.

P27   Kaplan, M.A., "Normative Controls on International Violence", in Boasson and Nurock (1973), 55-62.

P28   Kaplan, M.A., "Strategy and Morality", in Kaplan (1973), 13-38.

P29   Khadduri, M., "The Islamic Theory of International Relations and its Contemporary Relevance", in Proctor (1965), 24-39.

P30   Kirby, S., "National Interest *Versus* Ideology in American Diplomacy", in Benewick, Berki and Parekh (1973), 227-244.

P31   Kohn, H., "Freedom and Authority in International Relations", in Bryson, Finkelstein, MacIver and McKeon (1953), 103-108.

P32　Kraus, W.H., "Authority, Progress and Colonialism", in Friedrich (1958), 145-156.

P33　Lasswell, H.D., "The Major Trends in World Politics", in Lasswell and Cleveland (1962), 343-356.

P34　Lefever, E.W., "Morality versus Moralism in Foreign Policy", in Lefever (1972), 1-20.

P35　Lewis, H.D., "[My Lai:] The Non-Moral Notion of Collective Responsibility", in French (1972), 119-144.

P36　Mackinnon, D., "Natural Law", in Butterfield and Wight (1966), 74-88.

P37　Masters, R.D., "The Lockean Tradition in American Foreign Policy", in Farrell and Smith (1968), 69-93.

P38　Morgenthau, H.J., "Ethics and Politics", in Bryson, Finkelstein and MacIver (1947), 319-341.

P39　Munakata, I., "Towards New Cultural Relations in the International World: From Unilateral to Reciprocal Cultural Relations", in Boasson and Nurock (1973), 245-251.

P40　Murray, T.E., "Morality and Security: The Forgotten Equation", in Nagle (1960), 58-68.

P41　Neumann, W.L., "Ambiguity and Ambivalence in Ideas of National Interest in Asia", in DeConde (1957), 133-158.

P42　Neumann, W.L., "Determinism, Destiny, and Myth in the American Image of China", in Anderson (1959), 1-22.

P43　Nichols, J.H., "Reinhold Niebuhr: Prophet in Politics", in Krieger and Stern (1968), 370-386.

P44　Niebuhr, R., "The Social Myths in the 'Cold War'", in Farrell and Smith (1967), 40-56.

P45　Plamenatz, J.P., "What Principles Should Guide Us in Seeking to Influence Foreign Governments and Peoples?", in Lasswell and Cleveland (1962), 357-396.

P46　Price, H.B., "World Ethic and World Revolution", in Lasswell and Cleveland (1962), 397-407.

P47　Ramsey, P., "Force and Political Responsibility", in Lefever (1972), 43-73.

P48　Ramsey, P., "A Political Ethics Context for Strategic Thinking", in Kaplan (1973), 101-147.

P49   Rosenberg, C.E., "Anxiety, Ideology, and Order: Reflections on the Making of American Public Policy", in Barker (1971), 22-33.

P50   Rustow, D.A., "The Appeal of Communism to Islamic Peoples", in Proctor (1965), 40-60.

P51   Schlesinger, A., Jr., "National Interests and Moral Absolutes", in Lefever (1972), 21-42.

P52   Seton-Watson, H., "The Impact of Ideology [on international politics 1919-1969]", in Porter (1972), 211-237.

P53   Stern, G., "Morality and International Order", in James (1973), 133-155.

P54   Thompson, K.W., "Ethical Aspects of the Nuclear Dilemma", in Bennett (1962), 69-89.

P55   Thompson, K.W., "Isolationism and Collective Security: The Uses and Limits of Two Theories of International Relations", in DeConde (1957), 159-183.

P56   Thompson, K.W., "Norms and Realities in International Relations", in Rajan (1971), 83-93.

P57   Thompson, K.W., "Normative Theory in International Relations", in Farrell and Smith (1968), 94-108.

P58   Thompson, K.W., "Theology and International Relations", in Long and Handy (1970), 177-191.

P59   Verne, D.P., "Hegel's Account of War", in Pelczynski (1971), 168-180.

P60   Waltz, K.N., "Political Philosophy and the Study of International Relations", in Fox (1959), 51-67.

P61   Wight, M., "Western Values in International Relations", in Butterfield and Wight (1966), 89-131.

P62   Wittfogel, K.A., "Problems of Marxism and Relations Between the East and West", in Eissenstat (1975), 15-67.

P63   Wright, Q., "Equality in International Law and International Relations", in Bryson, Faust, Finkelstein and MacIver (1956), 335-366.

P64   Wright, Q., "The Relations of Universal Culture to Power Politics", in Bryson, Finkelstein and MacIver (1947a), 597-603.

P65   Wright, Q., "Sovereignty and International Cooperation", in Bains (1961), 14-37.

P66   Young, T.C., "Pan-Islamism in the Modern World: Solidarity and Conflict Among Muslim Countries", in Proctor (1965), 194-221.

Q - PEACE AND PACIFISM

Q1   Aranguren, J.L.L., "Openness to the World: An Approach to World Peace", in Hoffmann (1968), 191-207.

Q2   Balasubramanian, R., "The Technique of Nonviolent Resistance", in Ginsberg (1969), 297-309.

Q3   Boulding, K.E., "Toward a Theory of Peace", in Fisher (1964), 70-87.

Q4   Choucri, N., and North, R.C., "In Search of Peace Systems: Scandinavia and the Netherlands, 1870-1970", in Russett (1972), 239-274.

Q5   Deutsch, M., "A Psychological Basis for Peace", in Wright, Evan and Deutsch (1962), 369-392.

Q6   Etzioni, A., "International Prestige and Peaceful Competition", in Wright, Evan and Deutsch (1962), 226-245.

Q7   Etzioni, A., "Toward a Sociological Theory of Peace", in Gross (1967), 267-293.

Q8   Ferrell, R.H., "The Peace Movement [in the United States]", in DeConde (1957), 82-106.

Q9   Frank, J.D., "Human Nature and Nonviolent Resistance", in Wright, Evan and Deutsch (1962), 192-205.

Q10 Freeman, H.A., "Pacifism and the Law", in Ginsberg (1969), 284-296.

Q11 Freymond, J., "How the Small Countries Can Contribute to Peace", in Schou and Brundtland (1971), 177-185.

Q12 Galtung, J., "Peace Education and Peace Theory", in Boasson and Nurock (1973), 213-227.

Q13 Galtung, J., "Peace Thinking", in Lepawsky, Buehrig and Lasswell (1971), 120-153.

Q14 Harding, D.W., "The Concept of Peace", in Fletcher (1974), 252-261.

Q15 Keys, D.F., "The American Peace Movement", in McNeil (1965), 295-306.

Q16 Klineberg, O., "Alternatives to Violence: The Need for a New Way of Thinking about International Relations", in Tiselius and Nilsson (1970), 229-240.

Q17   Koenig, Monsignor H., "The Popes and Peace in the Twentieth Century", in Gurian and Fitzsimons (1954), 48-68.

Q18   Landheer, B., "Peace as an Engineering Problem: Implications of the Threat Society", in International Peace Research Association (1966), 140-145.

Q19   Martin, L.W., "Peaceful Settlement and Peaceful Change", in Wolfers, et al. (1966), 91-107.

Q20   Nikhilananda, S., "Peace: The Hindu View", in Ginsberg (1969), 243-259.

Q21   Röling, B.V.A., "The Limited Significance of the Prohibition of War", in Lepawsky, Buehrig and Lasswell (1971), 228-237.

Q22   Tucker, R.W., "Nuclear Pacifism: Some Reflections on the Community of Fear", in Barker (1963), 158-170.

Q23   Wright, Q., "Maintaining Peaceful Coexistence", in Wright, Evan and Deutsch (1962), 410-441.

R - INTERNATIONAL LAW

R1 Anand, R.P., "The Development of a Universal International Law", in Lepawsky, Buehrig and Lasswell (1971), 157-179.

R2 Anand, R.P., "Sovereignty of States in International Law", in Rajan (1971), 188-214.

R3 Aréchaga, E.J. de, "The International Court of Justice and the Judicial Settlement of International Disputes", in Jenks, et al. (1963), 54-63.

R4 Aréchaga, E.J. de, "International Responsibility of States for Acts of the Judiciary", in Friedmann, Henkin and Lissitzyn (1972), 171-187.

R5 Baade, H.W., "Individual Responsibility [in international law]", in Black and Falk (1972), 291-327.

R6 Bains, J.S., "Domestic Jurisdiction and International Law", in Bains (1961), 110-129.

R7 Barnet, R.J., "Toward the Control of International Violence: The Limits and Possibilities of Law", in Black and Falk (1971), 370-391.

R8 Bastid, S., "Have the U.N. Administrative Tribunals Contributed to the Development of International Law?", in Friedmann, Henkin and Lissitzyn (1972), 298-312.

R9 Baxter, R.R., "Ius in Bello Interno: The Present and Future Law", in Moore (1974), 518-536.

R10 Berman, H.J., "Soviet Law Reform and its Significance for Soviet International Relations", in McWhinney (1964), 3-17.

R11 Black, C.E., "Challenges to an Evolving Legal Order", in Falk and Black (1969), 3-31.

R12 Boals, K., "The Relevance of International Law to the Internal War in the Yemen", in Falk (1971), 303-347.

R13 Bos, M., "Intervention and International Law II", in Jaquet (1971), 69-75.

R14 Brownlie, I., "Humanitarian Intervention", in Moore (1974), 217-228. (see also R92)

R15 Bruce, W.J., "The United States and the Law of Mankind: Some Inconsistencies in American Observance of the Rule of Law", in Barker (1971), 85-110.

R16   Burke, W.T., "Ocean Sciences, Technology, and the Future International Law of the Sea", in Falk and Black (1970), 183-264.

R17   Caldwell, M.A., "Population [and the future of the international legal order]", in Black and Falk (1972), 32-67.

R18   Carey, J., "The International Legal Order on Human Rights", in Black and Falk (1972), 268-290.

R19   Chai, N.-Y., "Law as a Barrier to Change: A Korean Experience", in Barker (1971), 111-129.

R20   Corbet, P.E., "The International Definition and Protection of Human Rights", in Lepawsky, Buehrig and Lasswell (1971), 180-197.

R21   Corbet, P.E., "The Vietnam Struggle and International Law", in Falk (1971), 348-404.

R22   Davidson, E., "The Nuremberg Trials and One World", in Anderson (1959), 230-255.

R23   Deák, F., "Neutrality Revisited", in Friedmann, Henkin and Lissitzyn (1972), 137-154.

R24   Dean, A.H., "The Importance of International Law in the Maintenance of Peace", in Jenks, et al. (1963), 64-71.

R25   Deutsch, K.W., "The Probability of International Law", in Deutsch and Hoffmann (1971), 80-114.

R26   Dorsey, G.L., "Two Objective Bases for a World-Wide Legal Order", in Northrop (1949), 442-474.

R27   Eagleton, C., "The United Nations: A Legal Order", in Lipsky (1953), 129-142.

R28   El-Erian, A., "International Law and the Developing Countries", in Friedmann, Henkin and Lissitzyn (1972), 84-98.

R29   Elias, T.O., "The Expanding Frontiers of Public International Law", in Jenks, et al. (1963), 97-104.

R30   Elias, T.O., "Modern Sources of International Law", in Friedmann, Henkin and Lissitzyn (1972), 34-69.

R31   Emerson, R., "The New Higher Law of Anti-colonialism", in Deutsch and Hoffmann (1971), 203-230.

R32   Falk, R.A., "Confrontation Diplomacy [and international law]: Indonesia's Campaign to Crush Malaysia", in Scheinman and Wilkinson (1968), 127-174.

R33   Falk, R.A., "The Interplay of Westphalia and Charter Conceptions of International Legal Order", in Falk and Black (1969), 32-70.

R34   Falk, R.A., "Introduction [to the international law of civil war]", in Falk (1971), 1-29.

R35   Falk, R.A., "Janus Tormented: The International Law of Internal War", in Rosenau (1964), 185-248.

R36   Falk, R.A., "New Approaches to the Study of International Law", in Kaplan (1968), 357-380.

R37   Falk, R.A., "The Relevance of Political Context to the Nature and Functioning of International Law: An Intermediate View", in Deutsch and Hoffmann (1971), 177-202.

R38   Falk, R.A., "Revolutionary Nations and the Quality of International Legal Order", in Kaplan (1962), 310-331.

R39   Farer, T.J., "Law and War", in Black and Falk (1971), 15-78.

R40   Fawcett, J.E.S., "The International Protection of Human Rights", in Raphael (1967), 119-133.

R41   Fawcett, J.E.S., "The Application of the European Convention on Human Rights", in Friedmann, Henkin and Lissitzyn (1972), 228-241.

R42   Fawcett, J.E.S., "Human Rights and International Relations", in Morgan (1972), 17-36.

R43   Firmage, E.B., "Summary and Interpretation [the international law of civil war]", in Falk (1971), 405-428.

R44   Fisher, R., "Constructing Rules That Affect Governments", in Wright, Evan and Deutsch (1962), 342-354.

R45   Fraleigh, A., "The Algerian Revolution as a Case Study in International Law", in Falk (1971), 179-243.

R46   Fried, J.H.E., "International Law--Neither Orphan Nor Harlot, Neither Jailer Nor Never-Never Land", in Deutsch and Hoffmann (1971), 124-176.

R47   Fried, J.H.E., "The Universal Declaration of Human Rights: An International Effort at a Synthesis of Freedom and Authority", in Bryson, Finkelstein, MacIver and McKeon (1953), 451-459.

R48   Friedman, J.R., "The Confrontation of Equality and Equalitarianism: Institution-building Through International Law", in Deutsch and Hoffmann (1971), 231-287.

R49   Friedmann, W., "Human Welfare and International Law--A Reordering of Priorities", in Friedmann, Henkin and Lissitzyn (1972), 113-134.

R50   Friedmann, W., "Intervention and International Law I", in Jaquet (1971), 40-68.

R51   Friedmann, W., "The Relevance of International Law to the Processes of Economic and Social Development", in Falk and Black (1970), 3-35.

R52   Friedmann, W., and Collins, L.A., "The Suez Canal Crisis of 1956 [and international law]", in Scheinman and Wilkinson (1968), 91-126.

R53   Gerberding, W.P., "International Law and the Cuban Missile Crisis", in Scheinman and Wilkinson (1968), 175-210.

R54   Golden, J., "Force and International Law", in Northedge (1974a), 194-219.

R55   Goldie, L.F.E., "The Management of Ocean Resources: Regimes for Structuring the Maritime Environment", in Black and Falk (1972), 155-247.

R56   Gordenker, L., "Livelihood and Welfare [and the future of the international legal order]", in Black and Falk (1972), 248-267.

R57   Gottlieb, G., "The Nature of International Law: Toward a Second Concept of Law", in Black and Falk (1972), 331-383.

R58   Gros, A., "Concerning the Advisory Role of the International Court of Justice", in Friedmann, Henkin and Lissitzyn (1972), 313-324.

R59   Gros, A., "Peaceful Settlement of International Disputes -- Mediation and Conciliation", in Jenks, et al. (1963), 44-53.

R60   Gross, L., "The Development of International Law Through the United Nations", in Barros (1972), 171-217.

R61 Gross, L., "States as Organs of International Law and the Problem of Autointerpretation", in Lipsky (1953), 59-88.

R62 Gross, L., "The Right of Self-Determination in International Law", in Kilson (1975), 136-157.

R63 Guggenheim, P., "The Birth of Autonomous International Law", in Jenks, et al. (1963), 80-87.

R64 Guggenheim, P., "What is Positive International Law?", in Lipsky (1953), 15-30.

R65 Hammarskjöld, D., "Liberty and Law in International Life", in Jenks, et al. (1963), 22-31.

R66 Hazard, J.N., "Co-existence, Co-operation and the Common Law", in McWhinney (1964), 18-32.

R67 Hazard, J.N., "Coexistence Law Reconsidered", in Blegvad (1969), 191-204.

R68 Henkin, L., "The Once and the Future Law of the Sea", in Friedmann, Henkin and Lissitzyn (1972), 155-170.

R69 Herz, J.H., "The Pure Theory of Law Revisited: Hans Kelsen's Doctrine of International Law in the Nuclear Age", in Engel (1964), 107-118.

R70 Higgins, R., "The Desirability of Third-Party Adjudication: Conventional Wisdom or Continuing Truth", in Fawcett and Higgins (1974), 37-52.

R71 Higgins, R., "Internal War and International Law", in Black and Falk (1971), 81-121.

R72 Higgins, R., "International Law and Civil Conflict", in Luard (1972), 169-186.

R73 Higgins, R., "International Law and the UN System", in Morgan (1972), 37-62.

R74 Hoffmann, S., "International Law and the Control of Force", in Deutsch and Hoffmann (1971), 34-66.

R75 Hoffmann, S., "International Systems and International Law", in Knorr and Verba (1961), 205-237.

R76 Hoffmann, S., "A World Divided and a World Court Confused: The World Court's Opinion on U.N. Financing", in Scheinman and Wilkinson (1968), 251-273.

R77   Hula, E., "International Law and the Protection of Human Rights", in Lipsky (1953), 162-188.

R78   James, A., "Law and Order in International Society", in James (1973), 60-84.

R79   Jenks, C.W., "Law, Freedom and Welfare in Action for Peace", in Jenks, et al. (1963), 1-11.

R80   Jenks, C.W., "Multinational Entities in the Law of Nations", in Friedman, Henkin and Lissitzyn (1972), 70-83.

R81   Jessup, P.C., "The Challenge to International Law", in Bains (1961), 3-13.

R82   Jessup, P.C., "Untried Potentials of the International Court of Justice", in Lepawsky, Buehrig and Lasswell (1971), 215-227.

R83   Jones, E., "Nuremberg in Retrospect", in Boasson and Nurock (1973), 181-190.

R84   Kaplan, M.A., "Constitutional Structures and Processes in the International Arena", in Falk and Black (1969), 155-182.

R85   Kelsen, H., "The Essence of International Law", in Deutsch and Hoffmann (1971), 115-123.

R86   Khadduri, M., "Some Legal Aspects of the Arab-Israeli Conflict of 1967", in Lepawsky, Buehrig and Lasswell (1971), 238-264.

R87   Kimminich, O., "Peace Research and International Law", in Boasson and Nurock (1973), 229-243.

R88   Lachs, M., "Some Reflections on Substance and Form in International Law", in Friedmann, Henkin and Lissitzyn (1972), 99-112.

R89   Larson, A., "The Role of Law in Building Peace", in Wright, Evan and Deutsch (1962), 332-341.

R90   Lauterpacht, H., "Rules of Warfare in an Unlawful War", in Lipsky (1953), 89-113.

R91   Lillich, R.B., "Domestic Institutions [and international law]", in Black and Falk (1972), 384-424.

R92   Lillich, R.B., "Humanitarian Intervention: A Reply to Dr. Brownlie and a Plea for Constructive Alternatives", in Moore (1974), 229-251. (see R14)

R93   Lipson, L., "International Law", in Greenstein and Polsby (1975), Vol. 8, 415-435.

R94   Lissitzyn, O.J., "Sovereign Immunity as a Norm of International Law", in Friedmann, Henkin and Lissitzyn (1972), 188-201.

R95   Livingston, D., "Science, Technology, and International Law: Present Trends and Future Developments", in Black and Falk (1972), 68-123.

R96   Luard, E., "Conclusions [the international regulation of civil wars]", in Luard (1972), 215-229.

R97   Manning, C.A.W., "The Legal Framework in a World of Change", in Porter (1972), 301-335.

R98   McDougal, M.S., Lasswell, H.D., and Reisman, W.M., "The World Constitutive Process of Authoritative Decision", in Falk and Black (1969), 73-154.

R99   McNemar, D.W., "The Post-Independence War in the Congo [and international law]", in Falk (1971), 244-302.

R100 McWhinney, E., "Objectives and Method in International Law and the East-West Détente", in McWhinney (1964), 33-45.

R101 McWhinney, E., "Pax Metternichea: International Law and Power in the Era of the Détente", in Blegvad (1969), 335-349.

R102 Miller, L.H., "The Kashmir Dispute [and international law]", in Scheinman and Wilkinson (1968), 41-90.

R103 Moore, J.N., "Toward an Applied Theory for the Regulation of Intervention", in Moore (1974), 3-37.

R104 Morgenthau, H.J., "The Impact of the Cold War on Theories of International Law and Organization", in Said (1968), 176-184.

R105 Morgenthau, H.J., "The Impartiality of the International Police", in Engel (1964), 209-223.

R106 Munro, L., "Law and Outer Space", in Jenks, et al. (1963), 105-113.

R107 Neumann, W.L., "Law and Order in American Thought: An Ambiguous Heritage", in Barker (1971), 55-65.

R108 O'Brien, W.V., "Nuclear Warfare and the Law of Nations", in Nagle (1960), 126-149.

R109 O'Connell, D.P., "The Role of International Law", in Hoffmann (1968), 49-65.

R110 Padelford, N.J., "The Composition of the International Court of Justice: Background and Practice", in Deutsch and Hoffmann (1971), 288-327.

R111 Pal, R., "International Law in a Changing World", in Jenks, et al. (1963), 88-96.

R112 Pictet, J.S., "The Development of International Humanitarian Law", in Jenks, et al. (1963), 114-125.

R113 Plischke, E., "Sovereignty and Imperialism in the Polar Regions", in Lee and McReynolds (1949), 104-125.

R114 Pound, R., "Towards a New Jus Gentium", in Northrop (1949), 18-34.

R115 Raphael, D.D., "Equality, Democracy, and International Law", in Pennock and Chapman (1967), 277-287.

R116 Röling, B.V.A., "The Role of Law in Conflict Resolution", in de Reuck and Knight (1966), 328-350.

R117 Rommen, H., "The [Catholic] Church and Human Rights", in Gurian and Fitzsimons (1954), 115-153.

R118 Rosenne, S., "Bilateralism and Community Interest in the Codified Law of Treaties", in Friedmann, Henkin and Lissitzyn (1972), 202-227.

R119 Sabourin, L., "The Theory of the Four C's: Conflict, Coexistence, Competition, Co-operation - A Conjunctural Approach to International Law and Politics", in Boasson and Nurock (1973), 33-43.

R120 Samuels, S.T., "International Law and International Organization - The Benefits of Combined Study", in Boasson and Nurock (1973), 63-68.

R121 Scelle, G., "Some Reflections on Juridical Personality in International Law", in Lipsky (1953), 49-58.

R122 Scheinman, L., "The Berlin Blockade [and international law]", in Scheinman and Wilkinson (1968), 1-40.

R123 Schwarzenberger, G., "The Contribution of the Court of Justice of the European Communities to European Integration", in Engel (1964), 285-295.

R124 Sprout, H. and M.T., "The Ecological Viewpoint -- and Others", in Black and Falk (1972), 569-605.

R125   Starke, J.G., "The Primacy of International Law", in Engel (1964), 307-316.

R126   Starke, J.G., "Regionalism as a Problem of International Law", in Lipsky (1953), 114-126.

R127   Stone, J., "Approaches to the Notion of International Justice", in Falk and Black (1969), 372-460.

R128   Stone, J., "Of the Equality of Nations Doctrine and International Justice", in Blegvad (1969), 471-492.

R129   Sumida, G.A., "The Right of Revolution: Implications for International Law and World Order", in Barker (1971), 130-167.

R130   Tanaka, K., "Some Observations on Peace, Law, and Human Rights", in Friedmann, Henkin and Lissitzyn (1972), 242-256.

R131   Taubenfeld, H.J., "The Applicability of the Laws of War in Civil War", in Moore (1974), 499-517.

R132   Taubenfeld, H.J. and R.F., "Modification of the Human Environment [and the future of the international legal order]", in Black and Falk (1972), 124-154.

R133   Thomas, A.V.W. and A.J., Jr., "International Legal Aspects of the Civil War in Spain, 1936-39", in Falk (1971), 110-178.

R134   Tucker, R.W., "Legal Restraints on Coercion", in Wolfers, et al. (1966), 109-159.

R135   Tucker, R.W., "The Principle of Effectiveness in International Law", in Lipsky (1953), 31-48.

R136   Tunkin, G.I., "International Law and Peace", in Jenks, et al. (1963), 72-79.

R137   Van Dyke, V., "Violations of Human Rights as Threats to Peace", in Lepawsky, Buehrig and Lasswell (1971), 198-214.

R138   Verdross, A. von, "The Charter of the United Nations and General International Law", in Lipsky (1953), 153-161.

R139   Visscher, C. de, "Stages in the Codification of International Law", in Friedmann, Henkin and Lissitzyn (1972), 17-33.

R140   Vlasic, I.A., "The Relevance of International Law to Emerging Trends in the Law of Outer Space", in Falk and Black (1970), 265-325.

R141   Weston, B.H., "International Law and the Deprivation of Foreign Wealth: A Framework for Future Inquiry", in Falk and Black (1970), 36-182.

R142   White, I.L., "International Law", in Haas (1974), 251-269.

R143   Wilkinson, D., "The Article 17 Crisis: The Dispute over Financing the United Nations [and international law]", in Scheinman and Wilkinson (1968), 211-250.

R144   Willrich, M., "Civil Nuclear Power: Conflict Potential and Management", in Black and Falk (1971), 252-270.

R145   Wright, Q., "The American Civil War, 1861-65 [and international law]", in Falk (1971), 30-109.

R146   Wright, Q., "The Cuban Quarantine of 1962", in Stoessinger and Westin (1964), 179-213.

R147   Wright, Q., "Law and Politics in the World Community", in Lipsky (1953), 3-14.

R148   Wright, Q., "Non-military Intervention [and international law]", in Deutsch and Hoffmann (1971), 14-33.

S - INTERNATIONAL ORGANISATION

S1 Ago, R., "The State and International Organisation", in Jenks, et al. (1963), 12-21.

S2 Alger, C.F., "Interaction in a Committee in the United Nations General Assembly", in Singer (1968), 51-84.

S3 Alger, C.F., "Negotiation, Regional Groups, Interaction, and Public Debate in the Development of Consensus in the United Nations General Assembly", in Rosenau, Davis and East (1972), 278-298.

S4 Barros, J., "Introduction [to the United Nations]", in Barros (1972), 1-15.

S5 Bowett, D.W., "The Interrelation of Theories of Intervention and Self-Defense", in Moore (1974), 38-50.

S6 Buehrig, E.H., "A [United Nations] Charter Dilemma: Order Versus Change", in Lepawsky, Buehrig and Lasswell (1971), 265-279.

S7 Červenka, Z., "Major Policy Shifts in the Organization of African Unity, 1963-1973", in Ingham (1974), 323-342.

S8 Claude, I.L., "Domestic Jurisdiction and Colonialism", in Kilson (1975), 121-135.

S9 Claude, I.L., "The Growth of International Institutions", in Porter (1972), 281-300.

S10 Claude, I.L., "The United Nations and Collective Security", in Gray (1969), 108-126.

S11 Connell-Smith, G., "The Inter-American System: Problems of Peace and Security in the Western Hemisphere", in Gregg (1968), 47-90.

S12 Cox, R.W., "ILO [International Labour Organisation]: Limited Monarchy", in Cox and Jacobson (1973), 102-138.

S13 Cox, R.W., and Jacobson, H.K., "The Anatomy of Influence [in international organisation]", in Cox and Jacobson (1973), 371-436.

S14 Cox, R.W., and Jacobson, H.K., "The Framework for Inquiry [into decision making in international organisation]", in Cox and Jacobson (1973), 1-36.

S15   Cox, R.W., and Jacobson, H.K., "Power, Polities, and Politics: The Environment [of decision-making in international organisation]", in Cox and Jacobson (1973), 37-58.

S16   Dreier, J.C., "The Special Nature of Western Hemisphere Experience with International Organization", in Gregg (1968), 9-46.

S17   Evan, W.M., "Transnational Forums for Peace", in Wright, Evan and Deutsch (1962), 393-409.

S18   Fabian, L.L., "International Administration and Peace-keeping Operations", in Jordan (1971), 123-167.

S19   Franck, T.M., "Equality and Inequality of States in the United Nations", in Pennock and Chapman (1967), 306-313.

S20   Galtung, J., "Nonterritorial Actors and the Problem of Peace", in Mendlovitz (1975), 151-188.

S21   Ghebali, V.-Y., "The League of Nations and Functionalism", in Groom and Taylor (1975), 141-161.

S22   Goodrich, L.M., "The Changing United Nations", in Friedmann, Henkin and Lissitzyn (1972), 259-279.

S23   Goodrich, L.M., "The Role of the United Nations in the Promotion of Human Equality", in Bryson, Faust, Finkelstein and MacIver (1956), 367-378.

S24   Goodrich, L.M., "The UN Security Council", in Barros (1972), 16-63.

S25   Goodrich, L.M., "The United States, the United Nations, and the Changing World", in Rajan (1971), 129-143.

S26   Goodwin, G.L., "International Institutions and International Order", in James (1973), 156-187.

S27   Gordenker, L., "The Secretary-General [of the United Nations]", in Barros (1972), 104-142.

S28   Gregg, R.W., "Equality of States Within the United Nations", in Pennock and Chapman (1967), 288-305.

S29   Gregg, R.W., "UN Economic, Social and Technical Activities", in Barros (1972), 218-269.

S30   Groom, A.J.R., "Functionalism and World Society", in Groom and Taylor (1975), 93-111.

S31 Haas, E.B., "Collective Security and the Future International System", in Falk and Black (1969), 226-316.

S32 Haas, E.B., "Dynamic Environment and Static System: Revolutionary Regimes in the United Nations", in Kaplan (1962), 267-309.

S33 Haas, M., "International Administration", in Haas (1974), 271-300.

S34 Harris, Z.S., "A Language for International Cooperation", in Wright, Evan and Deutsch (1962), 299-309.

S35 Harrison, R.J., "Testing Functionalism", in Groom and Taylor (1975), 112-137.

S36 Hexner, E.P., "Teleological Interpretation of Basic Instruments of Public International Organizations", in Engel (1964), 119-138.

S37 Hoffmann, S., "Erewhon or Lilliput? - A Critical View of the Problem [of international military forces]", in Bloomfield (1964), 187-211.

S38 Jacobson, H.K., "The Changing United Nations", in Hilsman and Good (1965), 67-89.

S39 Jacobson, H.K., "ITU [International Telecommunication Union]: A Potpourri of Bureaucrats and Industrialists", in Cox and Jacobson (1973), 59-101.

S40 Jacobson, H.K., "WHO: Medicine, Regionalism, and Managed Politics", in Cox and Jacobson (1973), 175-215.

S41 Jacovides, A.J., "A View From Within: The Role of the Small States [in UN peace-keeping] and the Cyprus Experience", in Fawcett and Higgins (1974), 79-102.

S42 James, A., "The Security Functions of the United Nations", in Twitchett (1971), 82-109.

S43 James, R.R., "The Evolving Concept of the International Civil Service", in Jordan (1971), 51-73.

S44 Judge, A.J.N., and Skjelsback, K., "Transnational Associations and Their Functions", in Groom and Taylor (1975), 190-224.

S45 Kay, D.A., "The United Nations and Decolonisation", in Barros (1972), 143-170.

S46   Krause, L.B., and Nye, J.S., "Reflections on the Economics and Politics of International Economic Organizations", in Bergsten and Krause (1975), 323-342.

S47   Kriesberg, L., "U.S. and U.S.S.R. Participation in International Non-Governmental Organizations", in Kriesberg (1968), 466-485.

S48   Laves, W.H.C., "United Nations Assistance for Political Development: A Rationale", in Lepawsky, Buehrig and Lasswell (1971), 337-350.

S49   Lemass, S.F., "Small States in International Organizations", in Schou and Brundtland (1971), 115-121.

S50   Marshall, C.B., "Character and Mission of a United Nations Peace Force", in Wolfers, et al. (1966), 161-191.

S51   McKnight, A., "Functionalism and the Specialized Agencies", in Groom and Taylor (1975), 162-172.

S52   McNemar, D.W., "The Future Role of International Institutions", in Black and Falk (1972), 448-479.

S53   Merchant, L.T., "Control and Accountability of a United Nations Peace Force", in Wolfers, et al. (1966), 193-219.

S54   Michalak, S.J., "The United Nations and the League", in Gordenker (1971), 60-105.

S55   Miller, L.B., "International Organization and Internal Conflicts: Some Emerging Patterns of Response", in Gordenker (1971), 130-150.

S56   Morgenthau, H.J., "Political Conditions for a [n international military] Force", in Bloomfield (1964), 175-186.

S57   Morgenthau, H.J., "Political Limitations of the United Nations", in Lipsky (1953), 143-152.

S58   Nicholas, H., "An Appraisal [of international military forces]", in Bloomfield (1964), 105-125.

S59   Nye, J.S., "UNCTAD [United Nations Conference on Trade and Development]: Poor Nations' Pressure Group", in Cox and Jacobson (1973), 334-370.

S60   Potter, P.B., "International Administration: Factor for Human Unity or Discord?", in Bryson, Finkelstein and MacIver (1947), 173-183.

S61 Potter, P.B., "World Institutions", in Wright (1948), 259-266.

S62 Rana, S., "Afro-Asia: Its Political Credibility in the United Nations", in Rajan (1971), 144-163.

S63 Rostow, W.W., "International Organization and the Problem of Peace", in Mélanges Raymond Aron (1971), vol. II, 405-434.

S64 Schachter, O., "Interpretation of the Charter in the Political Organs of the United Nations", in Engel (1964), 269-283.

S65 Schachter, O., "Some Reflections on International Officialdom", in Fawcett and Higgins (1974), 53-63.

S66 Schachter, O., "The United Nations and Internal Conflict", in Moore (1974), 401-445.

S67 Scheinman, L., "IAEA [International Atomic Energy Agency]: Atomic Condominium?", in Cox and Jacobson (1973), 216-262.

S68 Schelling, T.C., "Strategy: A World Force in Operation", in Bloomfield (1964), 212-235.

S69 Schram, G.G., "The Role of the Nordic States in the U.N.", in Schou and Brundtland (1971), 123-127.

S70 Schwebel, S.M., "Wars of Liberation--as Fought in U.N. Organs", in Moore (1974), 446-457.

S71 Sewell, J.P., "Functional Agencies [and the future of the international legal order]", in Black and Falk (1972), 480-523.

S72 Sewell, J.P., "UNESCO [United Nations Educational, Scientific and Cultural Organisation]: Pluralism Rampant", in Cox and Jacobson (1973), 139-174.

S73 Smith, S.A. de, "Exceeding Small [small political entities and the U.N.]", in Fawcett and Higgins (1974), 64-78.

S74 Sohn, L.B., "The Growth of the Science of International Organizations", in Deutsch and Hoffmann (1971), 328-353.

S75 Stegenga, J.A., "United Nations Peace-Keeping: Patterns and Prospects", in Wood (1971), 299-314.

S76   Stoessinger, J.G., "Financing Peace-Keeping Operations", in Stoessinger and Westin (1964), 140-178.

S77   Strange, S., "IMF [International Monetary Fund]: Monetary Managers", in Cox and Jacobson (1973), 263-297.

S78   Stromberg, R.N., "The Riddle of Collective Security, 1916-1920", in Anderson (1959), 147-170.

S79   Symonds, R., "Functional Agencies and International Administration", in Jordan (1971), 98-119.

S80   Urquhart, B.E., "A UN Perspective [on international military forces]", in Bloomfield (1964), 126-144.

S81   Weiss, T., "Functionalism and International Secretariats: Ideology and Rhetoric in the U.N. Family", in Groom and Taylor (1975), 173-189.

S82   Wilcox, F.O., "International Confederation - The United Nations and State Sovereignty", in Plischke (1964), 27-66.

S83   Wood, R.S., "The League of Nations in Retrospect: Legal Doctrines and Political Conceptions", in Wood (1971), 59-68.

S84   Wright, Q., "Freedom and Authority in International Organization", in Bryson, Finkelstein, MacIver and McKeon (1953), 169-182.

S85   Wright, Q., "Specialization and Universal Values in General International Organization", in Bryson, Finkelstein and MacIver (1947), 207-217.

S86   Xydis, S.G., "The General Assembly [of the United Nations]", in Barros (1972), 64-103.

S87   Young, O.R., "The United Nations and the International System", in Gordenker (1971), 10-59.

T - INTERNATIONAL/WORLD ORDER AND INTEGRATION

T1 Aron, R., "The Anarchical Order of Power", in Hoffmann (1968), 25-48.

T2 Banks, M., "Charles Manning, the Concept of 'Order' and Contemporary International Theory", in James (1973), 188-209.

T3 Boulding, K.E., "Integrative Aspects of the International System", in International Peace Research Association (1966), 27-38.

T4 Bull, H., "War and International Order", in James (1973), 116-132.

T5 Bull, H., "World Order and the Super Powers", in Holbraad (1971), 140-154.

T6 Deutsch, K.W., "The Price of Integration", in Jacob and Toscano (1964), 143-178.

T7 Deutsch, K.W., "Transaction Flows as Indicators of Political Cohesion", in Jacob and Toscano (1964), 75-97.

T8 Earle, E.M., "National Power and World Order", in Woodward, et al. (1949), 137-165.

T9 Falk, R.A., "Reforming World Order: Zones of Consciousness and Domains of Action", in Laszlo (1973), 69-93.

T10 Falk, R.A., "Toward a New World Order: Modest Methods and Drastic Visions", in Mendlovitz (1975), 211-258.

T11 Falk, R.A., "The Trend Toward World Community: An Inventory of Issues", in Lepawsky, Buehrig and Lasswell (1971), 353-370.

T12 Falk, R.A., "World Revolution and International Order", in Friedrich (1969), 154-177.

T13 Falk, R.A., "Zone II as a World Order Construct", in Rosenau, Davis and East (1972), 187-206.

T14 Flugel, J.C., "Some Neglected Aspects of World Integration", in Pear (1950), 111-138.

T15 Fourastie, J., "Remarks on Conditions of World Order", in Hoffmann (1968), 286-299.

T16 Friedrich, C.J., "International Federalism in Theory and Practice", in Plischke (1964), 117-155.

T17 Gadamer, H.-G., "Notes on Planning for the Future", in Hoffmann (1968), 324-341.

T18 Goodwin, G.L., and Linklater, A., "Introduction: Changing Concepts of [world] Structure and Order", in Goodwin and Linklater (1975), 1-19.

T19 Haas, M., "International Integration", in Haas (1974), 203-228.

T20 Halpern, A.M., "The Revolution of Modernization in National and International Society", in Friedrich (1969), 178-214.

T21 Hayward, F.M., "Continuities and Discontinuities between Studies of National and International Political Integration: Some Implications for Future Research Efforts", in Lindberg and Scheingold (1971), 313-337.

T22 Hoffmann, S., "In Search of a New International Order", in Kuntz (1968), 355-372.

T23 Hutchins, R.M., "The Constitutional Foundations for World Order", in Woodward, et al. (1949), 95-114.

T24 Jacob, P.E., "The Influence of Values in Political Integration", in Jacob and Toscano (1964), 209-246.

T25 Jacob, P.E., and Teune, H., "The Integrative Process: Guidelines for Analysis of the Bases of Political Community", in Jacob and Toscano (1964), 1-45.

T26 Jaguaribe, H., "World Order, Rationality, and Socioeconomic Development", in Hoffmann (1968), 208-227.

T27 Jenkins, I., "Structure and Authority in International Relations", in Reigersman-van der Eerden and Zoon (1974), 5-9.

T28 Keohane, R.O., and Nye, J.S., Jr., "International Interdependence and Integration", in Greenstein and Polsby (1975), vol. 8, 363-414.

T29 Kothari, R., "World Politics and World Order: The Issue of Autonomy", in Mendlovitz (1975), 39-69.

T30 Lasswell, H.D., "Future Systems of Identity in the World Community", in Black and Falk (1972), 3-31.

T31 Lasswell, H.D., "World Loyalty", in Wright (1948), 200-225.

T32 Lindberg, L.N., "Political Integration as a Multidimensional Phenomenon Requiring Multivariate Measurement", in Lindberg and Scheingold (1971), 45-127.

T33 Lyon, P., "New States and International Order", in James (1973), 24-59.

T34 Malek, I., "World Order and the Responsibility of Scientists: A Functional as Opposed to an Institutional Approach", in Hoffmann (1968), 236-257.

T35 Mazrui, A.A., "World Culture and the Search for Human Consensus", in Mendlovitz (1975), 1-37.

T36 Mead, M., "World Culture", in Wright (1948), 47-56.

T37 Mendlovitz, S.H., "Models of World Order", in Gray (1969), 178-192.

T38 Mitrany, D., "A Political Theory for the New Society", in Groom and Taylor (1975), 25-37.

T39 Mitrany, D., "The Prospect of Integration: Federal or Functional?", in Groom and Taylor (1975), 53-78.

T40 Modelski, G., "World Order-Keeping", in Goodwin and Linklater (1975), 54-72.

T41 Modelski, G., "World Parties and World Order", in Falk and Black (1969), 183-225.

T42 Mus, P., "Buddhism and World Order", in Hoffmann (1968), 342-356.

T43 Northedge, F.S., "Order and Change in International Society", in James (1973), 1-23.

T44 Parsons, T., "Order and Community in the International Social System", in Rosenau (1961), 120-129.

T45 Parsons, T., "Polarization of the World and International Order", in Wright, Evan and Deutsch (1962), 310-331.

T46 Pentland, C., "Functionalism and Theories of International Political Integration", in Groom and Taylor (1975), 9-24.

T47 Plischke, E., "International Integration: Purpose, Progress, and Prospects", in Plischke (1964), 1-25.

T48 Sakamoto, Y., "Toward Global Identity", in Mendlovitz (1975), 189-210.

T49   Schwartz, B.I., "The Maoist Image of World Order", in Farrell and Smith (1967), 92-102.

T50   Smoker, P., "A Preliminary Empirical Study of an International Integrative Subsytem", in International Peace Research Association (1966), 38-51.

T51   Taylor, P., "Functionalism and Strategies for International Integration", in Groom and Taylor (1975), 79-92.

T52   Teune, H., "The Learning of Integrative Habits", in Jacob and Toscano (1964), 247-282.

T53   Teune, H., "Models in the Study of Political Integration", in Jacob and Toscano (1964), 283-303.

T54   Waddington, C.H., "The Desire for Material Progress as a World Ordering System", in Hoffmann (1968), 228-235.

T55   Weizsäcker, C.-F. von, "A Sceptical Contribution [on the World Order Models Project]", in Mendlovitz (1975), 111-150.

T56   Wirth, L., "World Community, World Society, and World Government: An Attempt at a Clarification of Terms", in Wright (1948), 9-20.

T57   Woodward, B., "Reason, Non-violence, and Global Legal Change", in Held, Morgenbesser and Nagel(1974), 154-196.

T58   Woodward, E.L., "The Historical and Political Foundations for World Order", in Woodward, et al. (1949), 9-34.

T59   Young, R., "Political and Legal Systems of Order", in Farrell (1966), 293-300.

U - THIRD WORLD, DEVELOPING AREAS, COLONIALISM, NON-ALIGNMENT

U1 Bienen, H., "Foreign Policy, the Military, and Development: Military Assistance and Political Change in Africa", in Butwell (1969), 67-111.

U2 Binder, L., "Egypt's Positive Neutrality", in Kaplan (1962), 175-191.

U3 Black, C.E., "The Relevance of Theories of Modernization for Normative and Institutional Efforts at the Control of Intervention", in Moore (1974), 53-69.

U4 Blanksten, G.I., "International Politics and Foreign Policy in Developing Systems", in Farrell (1966), 120-130.

U5 Burton, J.W., "Introduction to Nonalignment", in Burton (1966), 11-27.

U6 Burton, J.W., "Nonalignment and Stability", in Burton (1966), 62-98.

U7 Butwell, R., "Contemporary International Relations and Development", in Butwell (1969), 1-10.

U8 Casanova, P.G., "Internal and External Politics of Developing Countries", in Farrell (1966), 131-149.

U9 Choucri, N., "International Nonalignment", in Haas (1974), 123-149.

U10 Cohen, J.A., "China and Intervention: Theory and Practice", in Moore (1974), 348-379.

U11 Cowan, L.G., "Ghana's Fight for Independence", in Stoessinger and Westin (1964), 102-139.

U12 Cowan, L.G., "Political Determinants [of African Diplomacy]", in McKay (1966), 119-143.

U13 Degras, J., "The Communist Attitude Toward Colonialism (to 1941)", in London (1963), 19-33.

U14 Dinerstein, H.S., "Soviet Doctrines on Developing Countries: Some Divergent Views", in London (1963), 75-89.

U15 Emerson, R., "American Influence in Developed and Underdeveloped Countries", in Butwell (1969), 209-236.

U16   Emerson, R., "Colonialism Yesterday and Today", in London (1963), 3-18.

U17   Fatouros, A.A., "Participation of the 'New' States in the International Legal Order of the Future", in Falk and Black (1969), 317-371.

U18   Feierabend, I.K. and R.L., "Level of Development and Internation Behavior", in Butwell (1969), 135-188.

U19   Firmage, E.B., "The 'War of National Liberation' and the Third World", in Moore (1974), 304-347.

U20   Fleming, W.G., "Sub-Saharan Africa: Case Studies of International Attitudes and Transactions of Ghana and Uganda", in Rosenau (1969a), 94-121.

U21   Folson, B.G.D., "The Communist View of Colonialism --An African Interpretation", in London (1963), 45-55.

U22   Foltz, W.J., "Military Influences [in African Diplomacy]", in McKay (1966), 69-89.

U23   Good, R.C., "Colonial Legacies to the Postcolonial States", in Hilsman and Good (1965), 35-46.

U24   Gupta, S., "Great Power Relations and the Third World", in Holbraad (1971), 105-139.

U25   Heimsath, C.H., "Nonalignment Reassessed: The Experience of India", in Hilsman and Good (1965), 47-66.

U26   Hekhuis, D.J., and Youngblood, J.F., "The Nature of the Underdeveloped Areas", in Hekhuis, McClintock and Burns (1964), 29-40.

U27   Higgins, B., "Foreign Economic Policy and Economic Development", in Butwell (1969), 113-134.

U28   Hoselitz, B.F., and Willner, A.R., "Economic Development, Political Strategies, and American Aid", in Kaplan (1962), 355-380.

U29   Jensen, L., "Levels of Political Development and Interstate Conflict in South Asia", in Butwell (1969), 189-208.

U30   Kamarck, A.M., "Economic Determinants [of African Diplomacy]", in McKay (1966), 55-68.

U31   Khan, R., "The Problem of International Poverty: Is There a Legal Obligation on the Rich Countries to Help the Poor?", in Rajan (1971), 164-187.

U32 Kodzic, P., "Armaments and Development", in Carlton and Schaerf (1975), 202-211.

U33 Lagos, G., "The Revolution of Being [and the creation of a just world order]", in Mendlovitz (1975), 71-109.

U34 Laqueur, W., "'Neo-Colonialism'--the Soviet Concept", in London (1963), 34-44.

U35 Lin, P.T.K., "Development Guided by Values: Comments on China's Road and Its Implications", in Mendlovitz (1975), 259-296.

U36 Lowenthal, R., "'National Democracy' and the Post-Colonial Revolution", in London (1963), 56-74.

U37 Lystad, R.A., "Cultural and Psychological Factors [in African Diplomacy]", in McKay (1966), 91-118.

U38 McKay, V., "The Impact of Islam on Relations Among the New African States", in Proctor (1965), 158-193.

U39 McWilliams, W.C., "Political Development and Foreign Policy", in Butwell (1969), 11-39.

U40 Miller, J.D.B., "Fanon, Sartre, and the Third World", in Rajan (1971), 108-126.

U41 Morgenbesser, S., "Imperialism: Some Preliminary Distinctions", in Held, Morgenbesser and Nagel (1974), 201-245.

U42 Ness, G.D., "Foreign Policy and Social Change", in Butwell (1969), 41-66.

U43 Nicol, D., "Towards a World Order: An African Viewpoint", in Hoffmann (1968), 357-376.

U44 O'Brien, C.C., "Epilogue: Illusions and Realities of Nonalignment", in Burton (1966), 127-136.

U45 O'Leary, M.K., "Linkages Between Domestic and International Politics in Underdeveloped Nations", in Rosenau (1969a), 324-346.

U46 Onoe, M., "Some Factors in the Communist View of Neutrality", in London (1963), 90-98.

U47 Perroy, H., "The European Community and the LDCs [Less Developed Countries]", in Kohnstamm and Wolfgang (1973), 222-247.

U48   Pfeifenberg, W., "The Role of Neutrality in International Politics", in Boasson and Nurock (1973), 99-107.

U49   Pye, L.W., "The Underdeveloped Areas as a Source of International Tension Through 1975", in Hekhuis, McClintock and Burns (1964), 40-61.

U50   Rodney, W., "Neutralism and the West", in Erickson, Crowley and Galay (1966), 93-113.

U51   Rosenbaum, H.J., and Tyler, W.G., "South-South Relations: The Economic and Political Content of Interactions Among Developing Countries", in Bergsten and Krause (1975), 243-274.

U52   Rosenstein-Rodan, P.N., and Hekhuis, D.J., "Programs for Alleviating Instability [in the underdeveloped world]", in Hekhuis, McClintock and Burns (1964), 62-80.

U53   Said, A.A., "The Impact of the Emergence of the Non-West Upon Theories of International Relations", in Said (1968), 93-106.

U54   Sayegh, F.A., "Islam and Neutralism", in Proctor (1965), 61-93.

U55   Sayre, F.B., "Dependent Peoples and World Order", in Woodward, et al. (1949), 115-136.

U56   Schwartzman, S., "International Development and International Feudalism: The Latin American Case", in International Peace Research Association (1966), 52-77.

U57   Sohn, L.B., "Neutralism and the United Nations", in Wright, Evan and Deutsch (1962), 355-365.

U58   Taylor, T., "Force in the Relations Between Great Powers and the Third World", in Northedge (1974a), 146-165.

U59   Thorne, C.T., "External Political Pressures [on African Diplomacy]", in McKay (1966), 145-175.

U60   Townsend, M.A., "Hitler and the Revival of German Colonialism", in Earle (1950), 399-430.

U61   Vukadinović, R., "Small States and the Policy of Non-Alignment", in Schou and Brundtland (1971), 99-114.

U62   Waelder, R., "Protest and Revolution Against Western Societies", in Kaplan (1962), 3-27.

U63   Wallerstein, I., "Pan-Africanism as Protest", in Kaplan (1962), 137-151.

U64 Ward, B., "Problems of a Developing World", in Porter (1972), 264-280.

U65 Wolf, C., "Defense and Development in Less-Developed Countries", in Kaplan (1962), 381-387.

U66 Wriggins, W.H., "Political Development: Varieties of Political Change and U.S. Policy", in Hilsman and Good (1965), 113-126.

V - AREA STUDIES, REGIONALISM, REGIONAL INTEGRATION

V1   Alker, H.R., "Integration Logics: A Review, Extension, and Critique", in Lindberg and Scheingold (1971), 265-310.

V2   Alting von Geusau, F.A.M., "A Common Foreign Policy or Coordination of Foreign Policies: Problems, Implications and Prospects", in John (1975), 59-69.

V3   Alting von Geusau, F.A.M., "European Unification and the Changing International System", in Alting von Geusau (1974), 1-31.

V4   Barnet, R.J., "Regional Security Systems", in Gray (1969), 75-92.

V5   Beer, F.A., "Political-Military Regionalism and International Administration", in Jordan (1971), 168-186.

V6   Brundtland, A.O., "The Nordic Countries as an Area of Peace", in Schou and Brundtland (1971), 129-145.

V7   Burrows, Sir B., "European Security", in Kohnstamm and Wolfgang (1973), 128-151.

V8   Ceterchi, I., and Pomaizl, K., "Two Views from Eastern Europe [on sovereignty and integration]", in Ionescu (1974), 135-142.

V9   Chalmers, D.A., "Developing on the Periphery: External Factors in Latin American Politics", in Rosenau (1969a), 67-93.

V10 Claude, I.L., "The Enlarged [European] Community in a Changing International Environment", in John (1975), 1-19.

V11 Coombes, D., "'Concertation' in the Nation-State and in the European Community", in Ionescu (1974), 86-99.

V12 DeNovo, J.A., "American Relations with the Middle East: Some Unfinished Business", in Anderson (1959), 63-98.

V13 Desfosses, H., "Pessimism, Convergence, and Soviet African Relations", in Eissenstat (1975), 279-296.

V14 Donelan, M., "West Germany and Britain: The New International Environment", in Kaiser and Morgan (1971), 41-60.

V15 Dowty, A., "International Guarantees with Special Reference to the Middle East", in Carlton and Schaerf (1975), 215-230.

V16 Duchêne, F., "The European Community and the Uncertainties of Interdependence", in Kohnstamm and Wolfgang (1973), 1-21.

V17 Etzioni, A., "Atlantic Union, the Southern Continents, and the United Nations", in Fisher (1964), 179-207.

V18 Farrands, C., "The Regional Use of Force", in Northedge (1974a), 70-98.

V19 Frey-Wouters, E., "The Prospects for Regionalism in World Affairs", in Falk and Black (1969), 463-555.

V20 Frey-Wouters, E., "The Relevance of Regional Arrangements to Internal Conflicts in the Developing World", in Moore (1974), 458-496.

V21 Garnett, J.C., "Defence Collaboration in the European Community", in John (1975), 93-113.

V22 Gazzo, E., "The European Community and the United States", in Kohnstamm and Wolfgang (1973), 152-166.

V23 Gittings, J., "Touching the Tiger's Buttocks--Western Scholarship and the Cold War in Asia", in Morgan (1972), 220-248.

V24 Gladwyn, Lord, "World Order and the Nation-State--A Regional Approach", in Hoffmann (1968), 66-75.

V25 Haas, E.B., "The Study of Regional Integration: Reflections on the Joy and Anguish of Pretheorizing", in Lindberg and Scheingold (1971), 3-42.

V26 Hager, W., "The [European] Community and the Mediterranean", in Kohnstamm and Wolfgang (1973), 195-221.

V27 Hartshorn, J., "Europe's Energy Imports", in Kohnstamm and Wolfgang (1973), 104-127.

V28 Hassner, P., "Desirability, Objectives and Possibilities of a Common Ostpolitik", in John (1975), 125-143.

V29 Heathcote, N., "Neo-functional Theories of Regional Integration", in Groom and Taylor (1975), 38-52.

V30 Hoffmann, S., "Obstinate or Obsolete? The Fate of the Nation-State and the Case of Western Europe", in Hoffmann, (1968), 110-163.

V31   Holst, J.J., "The Changing Structure of Security in Europe", in John (1975), 21-36.

V32   Inglehart, R., "Public Opinion and Regional Integration", in Lindberg and Scheingold (1971), 160-191.

V33   Ionescu, G., "Between Sovereignty and Integration: Introduction", in Ionescu (1974), 7-24.

V34   John, I.G., "The Soviet Response to Western European Integration", in John (1975), 37-58.

V35   Kanet, R.E., "The Soviet Role in the Middle East", in Eissenstat (1975), 297-320.

V36   Kaser, M., "The Soviet Union and Eastern Europe", in Morgan (1972), 197-219.

V37   Kervyn, A., "Europe and the International Monetary System", in Kohnstamm and Wolfgang (1973), 51-81.

V38   Korbonski, A., "Theory and Practice of Regional Integration: The Case of Comecon", in Lindberg and Scheingold (1971), 338-373.

V39   Leifer, M., "The Limits of Functionalist Endeavour: the Experiences of South-East Asia", in Groom and Taylor (1975), 278-283.

V40   Luxemburgensis (pseud.), "The Emergence of a European Sovereignty", in Ionescu (1974), 118-134.

V41   Martin, L.W., "Europe and the Future of the Grand Alliance", in Hilsman and Good (1965), 17-34.

V42   Mathiason, J.R., "Old Boys, Alumni, and Consensus at ECLA [United Nations Economic Commission for Latin America] Meetings", in Merritt (1972), 387-404.

V43   McKay, V., "Research Needs [for African Diplomacy]", in McKay (1966), 177-210.

V44   Miller, E.H., "Canada, the United States and Latin America", in Lee and McReynolds (1949), 83-103.

V45   Miller, J.D.B., "Commonwealth Studies", in Morgan (1972), 136-155.

V46   Miller, L.H., "The Prospects for Order through Regional Security", in Falk and Black (1969), 556-594.

V47   Moore, J.N., "The Role of Regional Arrangements in the Maintenance of World Order", in Black and Falk (1971), 122-164.

V48   Muret, C., "The Swiss Pattern for a Federated Europe", in Earle (1950), 261-284.

V49   Nye, J.S., "Comparing Common Markets: A Revised Neo-Functionalist Model", in Lindberg and Scheingold (1971), 192-231.

V50   Nye, J.S., "Regional Institutions [and international law]", in Black and Falk (1972), 425-447.

V51   O'Leary, M.K., "The Nature of the Inter-American System", in Gregg (1968), 157-177.

V52   Pinder, J., "How Active Will the [European Economic] Community Be in East-West Economic Relations?", in John (1975), 71-91.

V53   Pryce, R., "The Politics of Co-operation and Integration in Western Europe", in Morgan (1972), 175-196.

V54   Puchala, D.J., "Internal Order and Peace: An Integrated Europe in World Affairs", in Ionescu (1974), 164-180.

V55   Puchala, D.J., "International Transactions and Regional Integration", in Lindberg and Scheingold (1971), 128-159.

V56   Rosenthal, G., "The EEC [European Economic Community] and the Maghreb", in Cordier (1971), 116-133.

V57   Russett, B.M., "Delineating International Regions", in Singer (1968), 317-352.

V58   Scheingold, S.A., "Domestic and International Consequences of Regional Integration", in Lindberg and Scheingold (1971), 374-398.

V59   Scheinman, L., "Economic Regionalism and International Administration: the European Communities Experience", in Jordan (1971), 187-227.

V60   Schmitter, P.C., "A Revised Theory of Regional Integration", in Lindberg and Scheingold (1971), 232-264.

V61   Tickell, C., "The Enlarged Community and the European Security Conference", in John (1975), 115-124.

V62   Tinker, H., "South Asia as a field of study in the West ", in Morgan (1972), 249-270.

V63   Wionczek, M.S., "Latin American Integration and United States Economic Policies", in Gregg (1968), 91-156.

V64   Wisniowski, J.A., "Problems of Political Equilibrium in the Soviet Proposals for a European Security Conference", in Cordier (1971), 151-174.

V65   Zeller, A., "European Agriculture and the World Economy", in Kohnstamm and Wolfgang (1973), 82-103.

V66   Zurcher, A.J., "The European Community - An Approach to Federal Integration", in Plischke (1964), 67-115.

W - ECONOMICS AND INTERNATIONAL POLITICS

W1 Alker, H.R., and Puchala, D.J., "Trends in Economic Partnership: The North Atlantic Area, 1928-1963", in Singer (1968), 287-316.

W2 Allen, W.R., "Cordell Hull and the Defence of the Trade Agreements Program, 1934-1940", in DeConde (1957), 107-132.

W3 Baldwin, R.E., and Kay, D.A., "International Trade and International Relations", in Bergsten and Krause (1975), 99-131.

W4 Bersten, C.F., Keohane, R.O., and Nye, J.S., "International Economics and International Politics: A Framework for Analysis", in Bersten and Krause (1975), 3-36.

W5 Berle, A.A., "Diplomacy and the New Economics", in Johnson (1964), 89-116.

W6 Boulding, K.E., "World Economic Contacts and National Policies", in Wright (1948), 95-100.

W7 Byrd, P., "Trade and Commerce in [Britain's] External Relations", in Boardman and Groom (1973), 173-199.

W8 Cooper, R.N., "Prolegomena to the Choice of an International Monetary System", in Bergsten and Krause (1975), 63-97.

W9 Curzon, V., and Curzon, G., "GATT [General Agreement on Tariffs and Trade] : Traders Club", in Cox and Jacobson (1973), 298-333.

W10 Diaz-Alejandro, C.F., "North-South Relations: The Economic Component", in Bergsten and Krause (1975), 213-241.

W11 Emery, F.E., "Economic Conflicts in Relation to War", in Wallace (1957), 40-66.

W12 Evans, P.B., "National Autonomy and Economic Development: Critical Perspectives on Multinational Corporations in in Poor Countries", in Keohane and Nye (1972), 325-342.

W13 Frank, C.R., and Baird, M., "Foreign Aid: Its Speckled Past and Future Prospects", in Bergsten and Krause (1975), 133-167.

W14 Gilpin, R., "The Politics of Transnational Economic Relations", in Keohane and Nye (1972), 48-69.

W15   Gilpin, R., "Three Models of the Future", in Bergsten and
        Krause (1975), 37-60.

W16   Goodwin, G.L., "Economics and International Politics", in
        Porter (1972), 238-263.

W17   Hoagland, J., and Teeple, J., "The Economics of Regional
        Arms Races", in Benoit (1967), 139-145.

W18   Hodges, M., "Functionalism and Multinational Companies",
        in Groom and Taylor (1975), 225-237.

W19   Holzman, F.D., and Legvold, R., "The Economics and Politics
        of East-West Relations", in Bergsten and Krause (1975),
        275-320.

W20   Kavanagh, D., "Beyond Autonomy? The Politics of Corpora-
        tions", in Ionescu (1974), 46-64.

W21   Keohane, R.O., and Ooms, V.D., "The Multinational Firm
        and International Regulation", in Bergsten and Krause
        (1975), 169-209.

W22   Krassowski, A., "The Aid Programme [in the management of
        Britain's external relations]", in Boardman and Groom
        (1973), 201-220.

W23   Krause, L., "Private International Finance", in Keohane
        and Nye (1972), 173-190.

W24   Lanyi, A., "Political Aspects of Exchange-Rate Systems",
        in Merritt (1972), 423-446.

W25   Linnemann, H., Pronk, J.P., and Tinbergen, J., "Conver-
        gence of Economic Systems in East and West", in Benoit
        (1967), 246-260.

W26   Mates, L., "International Trade and the Developing Coun-
        tries", in Burton (1966), 106-126.

W27   Mayall, J., "Functionalism and International Economic
        Relations", in Groom and Taylor (1975), 250-277.

W28   Miles, C., "International Economic Relations, II: Business
        and Trade", in Morgan (1972), 85-102.

W29   Morse, E.L., "Crisis Diplomacy, Interdependence, and the
        Politics of International Economic Relations", in
        Tanter and Ullman (1972), 123-150.

W30   Morse, E.L., "Transnational Economic Processes", in
        Keohane and Nye (1972), 23-47.

W31   Ogburn, W.F., "Introductory Ideas on Inventions and the State", in Ogburn (1949), 1-15.

W32   Peeters, T., and Hager, W., "The [European] Community and the Changing World Economic Order", in Kohnstamm and Wolfgang (1973), 22-50.

W33   Penrose, E., "International Economic Relations and the Large International Firm", in Penrose, Lyon and Penrose (1970), 107-136.

W34   Pye, L.W., "The Foreign Aid Instrument: Search for Reality", in Hilsman and Good (1965), 93-112.

W35   Rappard, W.E., "The Economic Foundations for World Order", in Woodward, et al. (1949), 77-93.

W36   Rosecrance, R., "International Interdependence", in Goodwin and Linklater (1975), 20-35.

W37   Strange, S., "International Economic Relations, I: The Need for an Interdisciplinary Approach", in Morgan (1972), 63-84.

W38   Sumida, G.A., "Transnational Movements and Economic Structure", in Black and Falk (1972), 524-568.

W39   Tinbergen, J.,"International Economic Planning", in Hoffmann (1968), 258-285.

W40   Vernon, R., "Multinational Business and National Economic Goals", in Keohane and Nye (1972), 343-355.

W41   Von Laue, T.H., "Problems of Modernization [in Russian foreign policy]", in Lederer (1962), 69-108.

W42   Wells, L.T., "The Multinational Business Enterprise: What Kind of International Organization?", in Keohane and Nye (1972), 97-114.

W43   Williamson, J., "Constraints on Economic Sovereignty", in Leifer (1972), 172-180.

X - SCIENCE AND TECHNOLOGY

X1   Brodie, B., "Military Technology and International Strategy", in Lepawsky, Buehrig and Lasswell (1971), 72-84.

X2   Brown, H.S., "Science, Technology and International Relations", in Brookings Institution (1956), 19-36.

X3   Buchan, A., "Technology and World Politics", in Porter (1972), 160-182.

X4   Fox, W.T.R., "Atomic Energy and International Relations", in Ogburn (1949), 102-125.

X5   Gilpin, R., "Has Modern Technology Changed International Politics?", in Rosenau, Davis and East (1972), 166-174.

X6   Haas, E.B., "An International 'Scientific Society'", in Goodwin and Linklater (1975), 73-85.

X7   Hampsch, G.H., "Technology in the Prospects for Peace: The View from Another Side [Marxist-Leninist ideology]", in Eissenstat (1975), 267-276.

X8   Hart, H., "Technology and the Growth of Political Areas", in Ogburn (1949), 28-57.

X9   Herz, J.H., "The Impact of the Technological-Scientific Process on the International System", in Said (1968), 107-126.

X10   Irish, M.D., "The Impact of Science and Technology Upon American Foreign Policy", in Said (1968), 127-159.

X11   Killian, J.R., "Science and Foreign Policy", in Johnson (1964), 57-87.

X12   Leigh, R., "The Mass-Communications Inventions and International Relations", in Ogburn (1949), 126-143.

X13   Malin, J.C., "The Contriving Brain as the Pivot of History: Sea, Landmass, and Air Power: Some Bearings of Cultural Technology upon the Geography of International Relations", in Anderson (1959), 339-363.

X14   Merchant, L., "New Techniques in Diplomacy", in Johnson (1964), 117-135.

X15   Ogburn, W.F., "Aviation and International Relations", in Ogburn (1949), 86-101.

X16   Ogburn, W.F., "The Process of Adjustment to New Inventions", in Ogburn (1949), 16-27.

X17   Oppenheimer, J.R., "The Scientific Foundations for World Order", in Woodward, et al. (1949), 35-51.

X18   Pokrovsky, G.I., "Improving the World: The Basis for Peaceful Coexistence", in Wright, Evan and Deutsch (1962), 278-286.

X19   Rock, V., "Science and Technology for an Interdependent World", in Benoit (1967), 228-236.

X20   Supek, I., "The Universality of Science: Our Last Hope", in Wright, Evan and Deutsch (1962), 294-298.

X21   Usher, A.P., "The Steam and Steel Complex and International Relations", in Ogburn (1949), 58-85.

X22   Williams, R., "Science, Technology, and the Future of Warfare", in Beaumont and Edmonds (1975), 157-179.

X23   Wright, Q., "Modern Technology and the World Order", in Ogburn (1949), 174-198.

AUTHOR INDEX

Abrams, P. G1
Abt, C.C. B1, N1
Ackoff, R.L. H74
Adamthwaite, A. C1
Ago, R. S1
Akzin, B. D1
Alexander, A.J. K1
Alexandrowicz, C.H. D2
Alger, C.F. A1, B2, H1, N2, S2,3
Alker, H.R. A2, B3, V1, W1
Alland, A. J1
Allen, W.R. W2
Allison, G.T. G2
Allott, A. D3
Allport, G.W. J2
Almond, G.A. G3
Alting von Geusau, F.A.M. V2,3
Anand, R.P. R1,2
Anderson, M.S. D4
Andrew, C. C2
Andrus, D. G102
Angell, R.C. H2, N3
Aranguren, J.L.L. Q1
Aréchaga, E.J. de R3,4
Aron, R. A3,4 P1, T1
Aspaturian, V.V. G4,5,6,7
Austen, R.A. C3,4
Avineri, S. F1

Baade, H.W. R5
Bader, W.B. L1
Baier, K. P2
Bains, J.S. R6
Baird, M. W13
Balasubramanian, R. Q2
Baldwin, R.E. W3
Ball, W.M. F2
Banks, M. T2
Barbu, Z. F3
Barghoorn, F.C. N4
Baring, A. G8
Barker, C.A. L2
Barnet, R.J. R7, V4
Barraclough, G. C5
Barros, J. S4
Barston, R.P. D5
Barzun, J. F4
Bastid, S. R8
Bates, S. P3
Baumont, M. C6

Baxter, R.R. R9
Bayandor, D. L3
Baynes, J.C.M. K2
Beaton, L. K3
Beaumont, R.A. H3
Bedau, H.A. J3
Beer, F.A. V5
Bell, C. D6, G9
Bell, J.B. E1, J4
Bell, P.D. E2
Bell, P.M.H. C7
Bellany, I. L4
Beloff, M. C8, E3
Bemis, S.F. C9
Benham, A.H. D11
Benington, H.D. K4
Bennett, E.M. M1
Bennett, J.C. J5
Benns, F.L. C10
Benson, O. A5, B4,5
Bergsten, C.F. W4
Berle, A.A. W5
Berman, H.J. R10
Besson, W. G10
Bethill, C.D. L5
Bienen, H. U1
Binder, L. U2
Birnbaum, K. L6
Birnbaum, N. G11
Bishop, D.G. G12
Bjøl, E. D7
Black, C.E. C11, G13, H4, R11, U3
Blake, N.M. C12
Blaker, J.R. K5, L7
Blanksten, G.I. G14, U4
Bley, H. C13
Bloch, C. C14
Blum, J.M. C15
Boahen, A.A. M2
Boals, K. R12
Boardman, R. G15
Bobrow, D.B. A6, B6,7, N5
Booth, K. K6
Bos, M. R13
Bossenbrook, W.J. F5
Boulding, K.E. D8,9, H5,6, Q3, T3, W6
Bouthoul, G. P4
Bowett, D.W. S5
Bozeman, A.B. P5
Brams, S.J. D10
Bremner, S. J86

141

Breuning, E. C16
Brinton, C. K7
Brodie, B. J6, K8, X1
Brody, R.A. A7,8,9, B8, D11, H36
Brogan, D.W. H7
Bronfenbrenner, U. H8
Brown, H.S. X2
Brown, N. K9,10
Brown, S.D. M3
Brownlie, I. R14
Bruce, W.J. R15
Brundtland, A.O. V6
Brunschwig, H. C17,18
Brzezinski, Z. G16
Buchan, A. D12,13, L8, X3
Buckley, T. M4
Buehrig, E.H. S6
Bull, H. A10, D14, P6, T4,5
Bundy, M. A11
Burhoe, R.W. D15
Burke, W.T. R16
Burks, R.V. E4
Burns, A.L. A12,13,14, D16, 49, K11, L9
Burns, R.D. M5
Burrowes, R. A15
Burrows, Sir B. V7
Burton, J.W. D17, H9,10,11, U5,6
Burtt, E.A. P7
Butler, J. C19
Butler, R. M6
Butler, W.E. G17
Butterfield, Sir H. D18, M7, 8, P8
Butwell, R. U7
Buzan, B. G18
Bychowski, G. G19
Byrd, P. W7
Byrnes, R.F. G20

Caldwell, M.A. R17
Cameron, E.R. M9
Carey, J. R18
Carmoy, G. de C20
Carpenter, C.R. J7
Carr, E.H. P9
Carroll, B.A. C21
Casanova, P.G. U8
Červenka, Z. S7
Ceterchi, I. V8

Chai, N.-Y. R19
Chalfont, Lord L10
Challener, R.D. M10
Chalmers, D.A. V9
Chang, P.H. K12
Chapman, J.W. K13
Chi, H.S. D19
Chilver, E.M. C22
Choucri, N. H12, Q4, U9
Chu, Pao-chin, M11
Clapp, P.A. N6
Claude, I.L. J8, S8,9,10, V10
Clemens, W.C. B9
Cohen, B.C. D20, G21,22, N7,8
Cohen, J.A. U10
Cohen, M. J9
Cohen, S.P. K14
Cohen, W.B. C23
Cole, C.W. P10
Coleman, D.C. J10
Coleman, J.S. F6
Collins, L.A. R52
Collins, R.O. C24
Connell-Smith, G. S11
Conroy, H. M12
Cook, W.G. N9
Coombes, D. V11
Cooper, D. P11
Cooper, R.N. W8
Coox, A.D. M13
Coplin, W.D. B10, M14
Corbett, P.E. R20,21
Coser, L. N10
Couloumbis, T.A. P12
Cowan, L.G. U11,12
Cox, R.W. S12,13,14,15
Craig, G.A. C25,26, K7,15, M15,16,17,18
Crane, R.D. K16
Crawford, R.M. J11
Cropsey, J. P13
Cross, M. F7
Crow, W.J. K93
Current, R.N. C27, P14
Curzon, G. W9
Curzon, V. W9

Daiches, D. L11
Dalkey, N.C. B11
Dallin, A. G23,24
D'Amato, A. P15
Davidson, E. R22

Davis, K.   D21
Davis, P.C.   C28
Davis, V.   K17
Davison, R.H.   M19
Davison, W.P.   N11
Deák, F.   R23
Dean, A.H.   R24
Deane, P.   J12
DeConde, A.   C29
Decornoy, J.   J13
De Forest, P.   see Forest, P. de
Degras, J.   U13
De Mello, L.M.B.   see Mello, L.M.B. de
DeNovo, J.A.   V12
Deschamps, H.   C30
Desfosses, H.   V13
De Smith, S.A.   see Smith, S.A. de
Deutsch, K.W.   A16, D22,23,24, E5,6,F8, G25,26, H13, J14, N12,13,14,15,16,17, Q5 R25, T6,7
Deutsch, M.   H14,15
De Visscher, C.   see Visscher, C. de
DeWeerd, H.A.   K18
Diamond, S.   J15
Diaz-Alejandro, C.F.   W10
Dicks, H.V.   F9, N18
Dinerstein, H.S.   D25, U14
Dion, L.   E7
Dodge, B.   F10
Donelan, M.   G27, V14
Dorsey, G.L.   R26
Dougherty, J.E.   J16
Downie, R.S.   P16
Dowty, A.   J17, V15
Dreier, J.C.   S16
Duchêne, F.   D26, V16
Duncan, W.G.K.   D27
Dunham, B.   J18
Dunn, D.   J19, P17
Duroselle, J.-B.   C31, G28, M20

Eagleton, C.   R27
Earle, E.M.   F11, J20, K19,20, T8
East, M.A.   D28, G29, H16
Eban, A.   M21

Edmonds, M.   J21,22
Eek, H.   E8
Ehrlich, S.   E9
El-Erian, A.   R28
Elias, T.O.   R29,30
Elkin, A.P.   J23
Elliott, P.   N19
Emerson, R.   R31, U15,16
Emery, F.E.   W11
Epstein, F.T.   H17
Epstein, L.D.   G30
Erickson, J.   K21
Etzioni, A.   Q6,7, V17
Evan, W.M.   S17
Evans, P.B.   W12
Eysenck, H.J.   J24

Fabian, L.L.   S18
Fage, J.D.   C32
Fain, H.   P18
Falk, R.A.   H18, J25, R32,33, 34,35,36,37,38, T9,10,11,12, 13
Farer, T.J.   R39
Farnsworth, L.   M22
Farrands, C.   V18
Farrell, R.B.   G31
Fatouros, A.A.   U17
Fawcett, J.E.S.   R40,41,42
Feierabend, I.K.   U18
Feierabend, R.L.   U18
Feiveson, H.   L12
Ferrell, R.H.   M23, Q8
Ficks, R.S.   K22
Field, J.A.   E10
Fieldhouse, D.K.   C33
Fifield, R.H.   C34
Figgures, F.   G32
Firmage, E.B.   R43, U19
Fischer, F.   C35
Fisher, R.   A17, G33, H19, R44
FitzGerald, C.P.   D29
Flack, M.J.   M24
Fleming, W.G.   U20
Flugel, J.C.   T14
Folson, B.G.D.   U21
Foltz, W.J.   U22
Ford, F.L.   M25,26
Forest, P. de   G34
Fourastie, J.   T15
Fowler, W.A.   G102
Fox, W.T.R.   A18,19,20, D30, X4

Fraleigh, A.   R45
Franck, T.M.   G35, S19
Frank, C.R.   W13
Frank, J.D.   L13, Q9
Frank, R.   J78
Franke, W.   D31
Frankel, C.   N20
Frankel, J.   G36
Free, L.A.   N21,22
Freeman, H.A.   Q10
Freeman-Grenville, G.S.P.
   C36
French, P.A.   P19
French, S.   F12
Freymond, J.   Q11
Freyre, G.   A21
Frey-Wouters, E.   V19,20
Fried, J.H.E.   R46,47
Friedman, J.R.   D32, R48
Friedmann, W.   R49,50,51,52
Friedrich, C.J.   G37, J26,
   T16
Frohlich, N.   G38
Fromm, E.   L14,15
Frondizi, R.   J27
Furet, F.   C37
Fuss, P.   J28

Gadamer, H-G.   T17
Galay, N.   K23
Galtung, J.   A22,23, G39, L16,
   Q12,13, S20
Gamson, W.A.   H20
Ganiage, J.   C38
Garder, M.   K24
Gardinier, D.E.   C39,40
Garnett, J.C.   A33, V21
Garthoff, R.   C41, K25,26
Gazzo, E.   V22
Gehlen, M.P.   G40
Geiger, T.   N23
Genova, A.C.   J29
Gerberding, W.P.   R53
Gersòn, L.L.   F13
Gewirth, A.   J30
Ghebali, V-Y.   S21
Gibb, H.A.R.   P20
Gibbs, N.   K27
Gibson, I.M.   K28
Gifford, P.   C42,43
Gilbert, F.   C44, K7,29, M27,
   28

Gillard, D.R.   C45
Gilpin, R.   W14,15, X5
Gittings, J.   V23
Gladwyn, Lord   V24
Glass, H.B.   J31
Glazer, N.   N24
Glennon, J.P.   K30
Gohlert, E.W.   K31
Golden, J.   D33, R54
Goldie, L.F.E.   R55
Golding, P.   N19
Good, R.C.   P21, U23
Goodrich, L.M.   S22,23,24,25
Goodwin, G.L.   A24, E11, P22,
   S26, T18, W16
Gorden, M.   B1,12
Gordenker, L.   R56, S27
Gordon, D.C.   C46
Gottlieb, G.   R57
Gottmann, J.   K32
Gough, K.   E12
Gray, C.   K33
Graymer, L.   D34
Green, P.   K34
Greene, F.   G41
Greenwood, D.   K35
Greer, S.   G42
Gregg, R.W.   S28,29
Gregory, F.   K36
Grinspoon, L.   G43, J32
Groom, A.J.R.   G15, S30
Gros, A.   R58,59
Gross, L.   R60,61,62
Guelke, A.   H21
Guerlac, H.   K37
Guetzkow, H.   B13,14,15,16,17,
   M54
Guggenheim, P.   R63,64
Guillen, P.   C47
Gupta, S.   L17, U24
Gurr, T.R.   G44
Gurtov, M.   G45
Gutman, A.   F12

Haas, E.B.   S31,32, V25, X6
Haas, M.   A25,26,27,28, H22,
   23,24,25, S33, T19
Habicht, M.   H26
Hager, W.   V26, W32
Haines, R.L.   D35,36
Hall, H.D.   C48
Halperin, M.H.   N6

144

Halperin, S.W. C49
Halpern, A.M. G46, T20
Hambro, E. M29
Hammarskjöld, D. R65
Hammond, P.Y. K38, L18
Hampsch, G.H. X7
Handel, M.I. K39
Hansen, R.D. N23
Harding, D.W. Q14
Harding, H. K40
Harf, J.E. G47, H27
Hargreaves, J.D. C50
Harris, J. J33
Harris, S.A. G22
Harris, Z.S. S34
Harrison, H.V. A29
Harrison, R.J. S35
Harrod, J. G48
Hart, H. X8
Hartman, R.S. J34
Hartshorn, J. V27
Harva, U. J35
Hassner, P. V28
Hatfield, M.O. J36
Hayward, F.M. T21
Hazard, J.N. R66,67
Head, R.G. K41
Heathcote, N. V29
Heimsath, C.H. U25
Heinlein, J.J. K42
Hekhuis, D.J. D49, U26,52
Held, V. P23
Henkin, L. R68
Heradstveit, D. J37
Hermann, C.F. G29,49,50, H28, 29,30,31,69
Hermann, M.G. G51, H69
Herriott, R.M. J38
Herz, J.H. K43, R69, X9
Hess, R.L. C51
Heston, E.L. M30
Heussler, R. C52
Hexner, E.P. S36
Higgins, B. U27
Higgins, R. R70,71,72,73
Hilsman, R. G52
Hinsley, F.H. C53, E13, F14
Hirsch, F.E. G53
Hoagland, J. W17
Hodges, M. W18
Hodgkin, T. M31
Hoffmann, S. D37, G54, H32, L19, R74,75,76, S37, T22,V30

Hoggard, G.D. A30, G117
Holborn, H. C54, K44, M32
Holbraad, C. D38
Holcombe, A.N. G55
Holloway, D. G56
Holloway, R.L. H33
Holst, J.J. D39, V31
Holsti, O.R. D40, G57, H34, 35,36
Holt, R.T. E14
Holzman, F.D. W19
Hoole, F.W. A31
Hoovler, D.G. G47
Hopmann, P.T. L20
Horkheimer, M. J39
Horelick, A.L. K45
Horner, C. L21
Hoselitz, B.F. U28
Howard, M. J40, K46,47,48, L22
Hudson, G.F. D41, K49
Hughes, H.S. M33
Huizenga, J. M34
Hula, E. R77
Hurewitz, J.C. K50
Hutchins, R.M. T23
Hyer, P. M35

Iklé, F.C. M36
Iliffe, J. C55
Ingham, K. C56
Inglehart, R. V32
Inglis, D.R. J41,42, L23
Ionescu, G. V33
Irish, M.D. X10
Iriye, A. N25
Isaacs, H.R. N26

Jackson, R. P24
Jacob, P.E. T24,25
Jacobson, H.K. S13,14,15,38, 39,40
Jacovides, A.J. S41
Jaguaribe, H. T26
James, A. E15, R78, S42
James, R.R. S43
James, T.E. G47
Janis, I.L. N27
Janowitz, M. J43, N28
Janssen, K-H. C57
Jenkins, B.M. J44

Jenkins, I.   T27
Jenks, C.W.   R79,80
Jensen, L.   E16, G58, U29
Jervis, R.   A32, M37, N29
Jessup, P.C.   R81,82
John, I.G.   A33, V34
Johnson, D.   C58
Johnson, J.E.   G59
Jonas, M.   C59
Jones, E.   R83
Joynt, C.B.   H37
Judge, A.J.N.   S44

Kahn, H.   A34, K51,52,53
Kaiser, K.   D42, E17,18, G60
Karmarck, A.M.   U30
Kamenka, E.   F15
Kanet, R.E.   V35
Kanter, A.   K54
Kanya-Forstner, A.S.   C60
Kaplan, M.A.   A35,36,37, B18, D24,43,44,45, G61, J45, K55,56, P25,26,27,28, R84
Kaser, M.   V36
Kaspi, A.   C61
Katz, D.   H38,86
Kaufmann, W.W.   M38
Kavanagh, D.   W20
Kavic, L.J.   K57
Kay, D.A.   S45, W3
Kecskemeti, P.   N30
Keenleyside, H.L.   G62
Kelly, J.B.   C62
Kelman, H.C.   A38,39, F16, H39
Kelsen, H.   R85
Kemp, A.   M39
Kemp, G.   K58
Keohane, R.O.   T28, W4,21
Kerr, M.   J46
Kervyn, A.   V37
Keys, D.F.   Q15
Khadduri, M.   P29, R86
Khan, R.   U31
Killian, J.R.   X11
Kimminich, O.   R87
Kindleberger, C.P.   A40
Kinney, K.   K59
Kiralfy, A.   K60
Kirby, S.   P30
Kirk, G.   N31
Kirk-Greene, A.H.M.   M40
Kissinger, H.A.   G63, K61, M41

Kitagawa, J.M.   N32
Klineberg, O.   Q16
Knight, K.   G102
Knoll, A.J.   C63
Knorr, K.   A41, E19, K62,63
Koch, H.E.   H91
Koch, H.W.   C64
Kodzic, P.   U32
Koenig, Monsignor H.   Q17
Kohn, H.   F17, P31
Kolodziej, E.A.   K64
Korb, L.J.   K65
Korbonski, A.   V38
Kothari, R.   T29
Kramish, A.   L24
Krassowski, A.   W22
Kraus, W.H.   P32
Krause, L.   S46, W23
Kriesberg, L.   H40, S47
Kronenberg, P.S.   J47
Kurat, Y.T.   C65

Lachs, M.   R88
LaFeber, W.   C66
Lagos, G.   U33
Lambeth, B.S.   K66
Landheer, B.   A42, D46, Q18
Lang, B.   J48
Langsam, W.C.   F18
Lanyi, A.   W24
Lapter, K.   H41
Laqueur, W.   U34
Larner, C.   G64
Larson, A.   R89
Lasagna, L.   J49
Lasswell, H.D.   A43, G65, N33, P33, R98, T30,31
Laszlo, E.   D47
Latourette, K.S.   C67
Laue, T.H. von   M42
Lauterpacht, H.   R90
Laves, W.H.C.   S48
Lee, J.   J50
Lefever, E.W.   P34
Legvold, R.   W19
Leifer, M.   G66, V39
Leigh, R.   X12
Lemass, S.F.   S49
Lentner, H.H.   H42
Lepawsky, A.   A44
Lerner, D.   N34,35,36
Lesser, A.   J51

Levi, W. M43
Levine, E.P. K67
Levy, M.J. A45
Lewis, H.D. P35
Lieberman, E.J. H43
Lieberson, K68
Lilienthal, A.M. C68
Lillich, R.B. R91,92
Lin, Han-sheng, M44
Lin, P.T.K. U35
Lincoln, C.E. F19
Lindberg, L.N. T32
Linklater, A. T18
Linnemann, H. W25
Lipson, L. R93
Lissitzyn, O.J. R94
Livingston, D. R95
Livingstone, F.B. J52
Loewenberg, P. G67
Loewenheim, F.L. C69
Long, N.E. G68
Lönnroth, E. M45
Lough, T.S. L25
Louis, W.R. C70,71
Lowenthal, R. U36
Lowi, T.J. G69
Luard, E. H44, R96
Luvaas, J. K69
Luxemburgensis (pseud.), V40
Lyon, P. A46, G70, T33
Lystad, R.A. U37

Macartney, C.A. C72
Mackinnon, D. P36
Mackintosh, J.M. K70,71
Mackintosh, M. C73
MacLeod, K. J53
MacLeod, R. J53
Macridis, R.C. G71,130
Malek, I. T34
Malin, J.C. X13
Mancall, M. N37
Manning, C.A.W. R97
Manning, R. N38
Manuel, F.E. C74
Mapp, R.K. G72
Margolis, J. J54
Marshall, C.B. G73, S50
Marshall, D.B. C75
Martin, F.X. F20
Martin, L.W. Q19, V41
Masters, R.D. P37

Mates, L. W26
Mathiason, J.R. V42
Matloff, M. J55
Mayall, J. W27
Mayer, A.J. C76,77
Mayer, S.L. C78
Maynard, H. N39
Mazrui, A.A. T35
McClelland, C.A. A47,48, D48,
    H45,46,47,48,49
McClintock, C.G. D49
McClosky, H. N40
McClure, R.D. H92
McDougal, M.S. R98
McGowan, P.J. A49, G74,75
McIntosh, D. K72
McKay, V. H50, U38, V43
McKnight, A. S51
McLellan, D.S. G76
McNeil, E.B. H51,52,53
McNemar, D.W. R99, S52
McWhinney, E. D50, R100,101
McWilliams, W.C. U39
Mead, M. D51, F21,22, H54,
    J56, T36
Medlicott, W.N. C79
Meehan, E.J. G77
Mello, L.M.B. de J57
Melman, S. J58, K73
Mendlovitz, S.H. T37
Merchant, L.T. S53, X14
Merritt, J.N. L33
Merritt, R.L. C80, E20, N16,
    41,42
Merton, T. J59
Metraux, R. H54
Meyer, A.G. F23, H55
Michalak, S.J. S54
Miers, S. C81
Miksche, F.O. K74
Milbrath, L.W. G78
Milburn, T.W. H56, K75
Miles, C. W28
Millar, T.B. L26
Miller, E.H. D52, V44
Miller, J.A. C82
Miller, J.D.B. U40, V45
Miller, L.B. S55
Miller, L.H. R102, V46
Miller, W.E. G79
Millis, W. K76
Mills, E.S. L27
Milstein, J.S. H57, J60

Milward, A.S.   C83
Mishler, A.L.   N43
Mishler, E.G.   G80
Mitrany, D.   T38,39
Miwa, K.   N44
Modelski, G.   D53, J61,62, T40, 41
Moore, D.W.   G81,82
Moore, J.N.   R103, V47
Morgan, R.   A50,51, D54, G60
Morgenbesser, S.   U41
Morgenthau, H.J.   A52,53,54, D55, G83,84, P38, R104,105, S56,57
Moriarty, J.K.   K77
Morse, E.L.   W29,30
Morton, L.   C84
Moss, J.A.   F24
Mosse, G.L.   F25
Munakata, I.   P39
Munro, L.   R106
Munton, D.   G121
Muret, C.   V48
Murphy, G.   J63
Murray, T.E.   P40
Mus, P.   T42

Naess, A.   J64
Nailor, P.   J65, K78,79
Nairn, R.C.   J66
Nardin, T.   K103
Naroll, R.   A55, K80
Narr, W-D.   G85
Nef, J.   J67
Ness, G.D.   U42
Neu, C.E.   G86
Neumann, S.   K81
Neumann, W.L.   P41,42, R107
Nevakivi, J.   C85
Newbury, C.   C86,87
Nichol, D.   U43
Nicholas, H.   S58
Nichols, J.H.   P43
Niebuhr, R.   E21, P44
Nielsen, K.   G87
Nikhilananda, S.   Q20
Nish, C.   C88
Nish, I.H.   C89, G88
Nitze, P.A.   A56
Nobel, J.W.   M46
Noel, R.C.   B19,20
Nolutshungu, S.C.   G89

Norman, J.   N45
North, R.C.   A57,58, H12,35, 36,58,91, N46, Q4
Northedge, F.S.   G90,91, K82, T43
Nye, J.S.   E22,23, F26, S46, 59, T28, V49,50, W4

Oakeshott, M.   E24
Obichere, B.I.   C90
O'Brien, C.C.   U44
O'Brien, W.V.   R108
O'Connell, D.P.   R109
Oeser, O.A.   H59
Ogburn, W.F.   W31, X15,16
O'Leary, M.K.   G92,93, U45, V51
Olson, W.C.   A59
Onoe, M.   U46
Ooms, V.D.   W22
Oppenheim, A.N.   M47
Oppenheimer, J.A.   G38
Oppenheimer, J.R.   X17
Ørvik, N.   C91, K83
Osgood, C.E.   L28
Osgood, R.E.   D56, K84, L29

Padelford, N.J.   R110
Padover, S.K.   A60
Paige, G.D.   H60
Pal, R.   R111
Palmer, R.R.   K85
Paret, P.   C92, K86
Park, R.L.   G94
Parsons, H.L.   J68
Parsons, T.   T44,45
Passin, H.   G95
Paul, B.D.   J69
Pear, T.H.   J70
Peardon, T.P.   F27
Peeters, T.   W32
Pender-Cudlip, P.   C93
Pendill, C.G.   G96
Penrose, E.F.   D57, W33
Penson, Dame L.M.   C94
Pentland, C.   T46
Perkins, D.   N47
Perroy, H.   U47
Peterson, P.A.   K87
Peterson, S.   N48
Pfeifenberg, W.   U48

Phillips, W.R.   N49
Pickles, D.   G97
Pictet, J.S.   R112
Pinder, J.   V52
Pipes, R.E.   G98,99
Plamenatz, J.   F28, P45
Plischke, E.   G100, M48, R113, T47
Pogue, F.C.   C95
Pokrovsky, G.I.   X18
Pomaizl, K.   V8
Pool, I.d.S.   K88, N1,50,51, 52
Possony, S.T.   K89
Potholm, C.P.   G101
Potter, P.B.   S60,61
Poullada, L.B.   M49
Pound, R.   R114
Powell, C.A.   G102
Price, H.B.   P46
Proebst, H.   C96
Pronk, J.P.   W25
Pruitt, D.G.   N53
Pryce, R.   V53
Puchala, D.J.   A61, V54,55, W1
Pye, L.W.   U49, W35

Qadir, C.A.   J71
Quandt, R.E.   B21
Quester, G.H.   D58, K90

Radway, L.I.   J72
Ramazani, R.K.   C97
Ramm, A.   C98
Ramsey, P.   J73, P47,48
Rana, S.   S62
Ranger, R.   G103
Ransom, H.H.   A62
Raphael, D.D.   R115
Rapoport, A.   A63, B22,23, D59, H61,62,63,64, K91, N54
Rappard, W.E.   W35
Raser, J.R.   K92,93
Read, T.   K94
Rees, D.   K95
Reinken, D.L.   D60
Reisman, M.   J74
Reisman, W.M.   H65, R98
Reveley, W.T.III,   G104

Reynolds, P.A.   D61,62
Richards, P.G.   G105
Richardson, J.L.   D63
Richardson, L.F.   H66, J75
Richman, A.   N55
Rickman, J.   J76
Riggs, F.W.   D64
Roberts, A.   H67
Roberts, H.L.   G106, M50,51
Robinson, J.A.   G107,108, H68, 69
Rock, V.   X19
Rodney, W.   U50
Roherty, J.M.   K96
Röling, B.V.A.   Q21, R116
Rommen, H.   R117
Ropp, T.   K97
Rose, P.I.   F29
Rosecrance, R.N.   M52, W36
Rosen, S.   D65, J77,78, K98
Rosenau, J.N.   A41, E25,26, F30, G109,110,111,112,113, 114,115,116,117, J79,80
Rosenbaum, H.J.   U51
Rosenberg, C.E.   P49
Rosenberg, M.J.   N56,57
Rosenne, S.   R118
Rosenstein-Rodan, P.N.   U52
Rosenthal, G.   V56
Ross, G.   M53
Rostow, W.W.   G118, S63
Rotberg, R.I.   C99
Rothfels, H.   C100, K99
Rowe, D.N.   F31
Rubinstein, A.Z.   G119
Ruebensaal, J.D.   K100
Rummel, R.J.   B24, G120, H70, 71
Russell, B.   C101
Russett, B.M.   A64,65,66, D66, K101, N58,59, V57
Rustow, D.A.   P50

Sabourin, L.   R119
Saeki, S.   N60
Said, A.A.   A67, U53
Sainsbury, K.   C102
Sakamoto, Y.   T48
Salmore, S.A.   G121
Sampson, A.   G122
Samuels, S.T.   R120
Sanderson, G.N.   C103

Sapin, B.M.   G123
Sargeant, H.H.   N61
Saul, L.J.   N62
Sawyer, J.   M54
Sayegh, F.A.   U54
Sayre, F.B.   U55
Scalapino, R.A.   G124
Scelle, G.   R121
Schachter, O.   S64,65,66
Scheingold, S.A.   V58
Scheinman, L.   R122, S67, V59
Schelling, T.C.   B25,26, K102, S68
Schiebel, J.   G125
Schiller, H.I.   N63
Schilpp, P.A.   E27
Schlesinger, A.   C104, P51
Schmitt, B.E.   C105, N64
Schmitt, H.O.   E28
Schmitter, P.C.   V60
Schmokel, W.W.   C106
Schorske, C.E.   M26,55
Schram, G.G.   S69
Schuman, F.L.   F32
Schwartz, B.I.   T49
Schwartz, D.C.   H72
Schwartzman, S.   U56
Schwarz, H-P.   D67
Schwarz, U.   C107, L30
Schwarzenberger, G.   R123
Schwebel, S.M.   S70
Schweigler, G.L.   G26
Scott, A.M.   J81
Scott, J.   G126
Scott, W.A.   N65
Scott, W.E.   C108, D68
Seabury, P.   F33
Sears, L.M.   C109
Senghaas, D.   J14, N17
Service, E.   J82
Seton-Watson, H.   P52
Sewell, J.P.   S71,72
Shalloo, J.P.   C110
Shanahan, W.O.   F34
Sharp, G.   J83
Shaw, T.M.   G127
Shepherd, G.W.   F35
Shinn, R.L.   J84
Shonfield, A.   A68
Shubik, M.   B27,28
Sibley, M.Q.   L31
Simpson, J.   K36
Simpson, S.   M56

Siney, M.C.   C111
Singer, J.D.   A69,70,71,72, D69, H73, J85,86,87, L32
Sisson, R.L.   H74
Skjelsback, K.   E29, S44
Skolimowski, H.   A73
Slagle, J.R.   B29
Slater, J.   K103
Sliwowski, G.   J88
Small, M.   N66
Smart, I.   M47
Smith, A.   C117
Smith, G.   C112
Smith, K.W.   L33
Smith, M.B.   N27
Smith, S.A. de   S73
Smoke, R.   K104
Smoker, P.   B30, T50
Snyder, G.H.   H75
Snyder, R.C.   A74, B31
Sohn, L.B.   S74, U57
Solomon, L.N.   B32
Somerville, J.   J89
Sommer, T.   L34
Sondermann, F.A.   A75
Speier, H.   K105, N67
Spiro, H.J.   D70, E30
Spits, Lt. Col. Drs. F.C.   J90
Sprout, H.   R124
Sprout, M.T.   K106, R124
Stagner, R.   H76
Stankiewicz, W.J.   E31,32
Starke, J.G.   R125,126
Stavrianos, L.S.   C113
Stegenga, J.A.   S75
Steinkraus, W.E.   J91
Stengers, J.   C114,115
Stern, F.   C116
Stern, G.   G128, P53
Stoessinger, J.G.   N68, S76
Stokes, W.S.   H77
Stone, J.   R127,128
Stourzh, G.   D71
Strandmann, H.P. von   C117
Strange, S.   S77, W37
Strassoldo, R.   E33
Stromberg, R.N.   S78
Stroup, M.J.   A76
Stuckey, J.   J86
Sullivan, H.S.   H78
Sullivan, J.D.   D40,72,73
Sullivan, M.P.   H79
Sumida, G.A.   R129, W38

Supek, I.   X20
Svala, G.   L35
Swanson, M.W.   C118
Symonds, R.   S79
Szalai, A.   J92

Talensky, N.   L36
Tanaka, K.   R130
Tandon, Y.   G129
Tanter, R.   A77, H80
Tatu, M.   D74
Taubenfeld, H.J.   R131,132
Taubenfeld, R.F.   R132
Taylor, A.M.   D75
Taylor, P.   T51
Taylor, T.   U58
Teeple, J.   W18
Temperley, H.W.V.   C119
Teters, B.   M57
Teune, H.   T52,53
Thieme, F.P.   J93
Thimme, A.   C120
Thomas, A.J., Jr.   R133
Thomas, A.V.W.   R133
Thomas, H.   C121
Thomas, W.   H79
Thompson, K.W.   A78,79,80,81, G130, P54,55,56,57,58
Thompson, L.   C122
Thorne, C.T.   U59
Thorson, S.J.   G131, K54
Tickell, C.   V61
Tillman, S.   N69
Timberlake, C.E.   M58
Tinbergen, J.   W25,39
Tinker, H.   V62
Törnebohm, H.   A82
Toscano, M.   C123
Townsend, M.A.   U60
Toynbee, A.J.   C124, J94
Trask, D.F.   G132
Trebilcock, C.   J95
Tucker, R.C.   D49, G133
Tucker, R.W.   Q22, R134,135
Tung, W.L.   H81
Tunkin, G.I.   R136
Turner, H.A. Jr.   C125
Turner, J.E.   E14
Twitchett, K.J.   K107
Tyler, W.G.   U51

Ulam, A.B.   F36
Urban, L.   L37
Urquhart, B.E.   S80
Usher, A.P.   X21

Vallier, I.   E33
Van Den Bergh, G.v.B.   F37
Vandenbosch, A.   F38
VanDeusen, G.G.   F39
Van Dyke, V.   R137
Varg, P.A.   C126
Vatikiotis, P.J.   G134
Vayda, A.P.   J96
Velvel, L.R.   G135
Verba, S.   G136
Verdross, A. von   R138
Verne, D.P.   P59
Vernon, R.   W40
Vigor, P.H.   J97
Vinson, J.C.   K108
Visscher, C. de   R139
Vital, D.   E35
Vlasic, I.A.   R140
Von Laue, T.H.   W41
Vukadinović, R.   U61

Wabeke, B.H.   N70
Waddington, C.H.   T54
Wadsworth, J.J.   M59
Waelder, R.   U62
Waite, R.G.L.   F40
Waites, N.   C127
Wakaizumi, K.   L38
Walker, R.L.   M60
Wallace, A.F.C.   J98
Wallace, M.D.   J99
Wallace, W.   G137
Waller, B.   C128
Wallerstein, I.   U63
Waltz, K.N.   A83, B33, D76, G138, H82, P60
Wang, G.   F41
Ward, B.   U64
Warner, E.   K109
Warner, E.L.   K110
Warner, G.   C129
Warwick, D.P.   E36
Waskow, A.I.   C130, H83
Wasserstrom, R.   J100
Watson, D.R.   C131
Watt, D.C.   C132,133,134,135

Wedge, B.   N71
Weinstein, M.E.   K111
Weisband, E.   G35
Weiskel, T.C.   C43
Weiss, T.   S81
Weizsäcker, C-F. von   T55
Welch, S.   N72
Wells, L.T.   W42
Weston, B.H.   R141
Whitaker, U.G., Jr.   A84
White, I.L.   R142
White, R.K.   H84, N73
Whiting, A.S.   G139,140
Whittlesey, D.   K112
Wight, M.   A85, D77,78, P61
Wilcox, F.O.   S82
Wilcox, W.   G141, K113
Wiles, P.   J101
Wilkenfeld, J.   A86, H90
Wilkes, D.   H85
Wilkinson, D.   R143
Willequet, J.   C136
Williams, A.   C137, J102
Williams, B.J.   C138
Williams, G.M.   F42
Williams, R.   X22
Williamson, J.   W43
Willner, A.R.   U28
Willrich, M.   R144
Wilson, A.   D79
Windsor, P.   G142
Winkler, H.R.   M61
Wionczek, M.S.   V63
Wirth, L.   T56
Wisniowski, J.A.   V64
Withey, S.   H86
Wittfogel, K.A.   P62
Wohlstetter, A.   A87, B34
Wolf, C.   U65
Wolfe, B.D.   H87
Wolfe, T.W.   K114,115
Wolfers, A.   E37, L39
Wolfowitz, P.D.   K116
Wood, H.J.   M62
Wood, R.S.   S83
Woodward, B.   T57
Woodward, E.L.   T58
Wriggins, W.H.   U66
Wright, M.   A33
Wright, Q.   A88,89, H88, N74,
   P63,64,65, Q23, R145,146,
   147,148, S84,85, X23
Wuorinen, J.H.   F43

Xydis, S.G.   S86

Yahuda, M.B.   G143
Yarmolinsky, A.   L40
Young, O.R.   A90,91, D80, E38,
   S87, T59
Young, T.C.   P66
Youngblood, J.F.   U26
Younger, K.G.   C139

Zahn, G.C.   J103
Zartman, I.W.   G144
Zasloff, J.J.   J104
Zechlin, E.   C140
Zeller, A.   V65
Zinner, P.E.   M63
Zinnes, D.A.   A92,93, G145,
   H89,90,91,92
Zinnes, J.L.   H92
Zurcher, A.J.   V66

SUBJECT INDEX

Aberystwyth A33
Acheson, Dean G76,114
Actors (Section E) A84, G22,
 J74, N14, P5, R93, S20
Adenauer, Konrad G10,53,100
Administrative tribunals R8
Advertising N63
Africa C4,17,18,19,22,23,24,
 30,32,33,38,40,42,43,47,50,
 51,52,55,56,60,61,63,67,70,
 71,75,81,86,87,90,99,103,
 112,122,136, F6,26, G127,
 129,144, H50, M40, R29, S7,
 V43
 boundaries of D3
 communism in F42
 diplomacy of C36,56,93,
 M2,31,40
 East C36
 foreign services of M40
 and France C17,33,115,122
 and Germany C13
 nationalism in F6,26
 partition of D2
 and Portugal C136
 pre-colonial C36,93, M2,31
 Southern R137
 and Soviet Union V13
 and United Kingdom C33,115,
 122
 See also Section U; and
 individual countries
Afro-Arab relations U38
Afro-Asian relations S62,
 U43
Afro-German relations C13
Aggression H33,52,59,84, J7,
 23,24,39,64,70,76,92,93,
 N62, Q5,9,16. See also
 Anthropology; Human Nature
Agriculture J50
Air power K109, X15
Algeciras Conference C78
Algeria C46, R45, V56
 and France C46
Alignments, informal D72.
 See also Blocs
Alliances (Section D) C2,7,
 8, 65,102, G47, J87, K30,
 72, V5,18,31. See also
 Blocs; North Atlantic
 Treaty Organisation
Allied occupation policy G100

Anglo-French Union Project
 C8
Anglo-German Naval Agreement
 C14
Anglo-Japanese Alliance C89
Antarctic R113
Anthropology H33,54,59, J7,
 23,51,52,56,70,82,93,96,
 T36. See also Aggression;
 Human Nature
Anti-ballistic missiles L36,
 X1
Anti-colonialism F7, R48,
 S8, U62,63. See also Colo-
 nialism; Decolonisation;
 Neo-colonialism; Post-
 colonialism
Anti-Semitism F40
Apartheid R137. See also
 South Africa
Arab-Israeli war 1967 J37,
 R86, V15,35. See also
 Israel; Middle East;
 United Nations
Arctic R113
Armaments H66, J99, L32.
 See also Weapons
Arms control (Section L)
 K101, R44, U32, X10. See
 also Disarmament; Proli-
 feration, nuclear
Arms races K50,51,90,110,
 L4,12,23,31, W17
Aron, Raymond A80,90
Asia F31,41, G125, M60, N32,
 37, P42,62, V23
 politics of U25
 study of international re-
 lations in V62
 and United States C34,89,
 P41, V23
 See also South Asia;
 South-East Asia; and indi-
 vidual countries
Atlantic community P12, V4.
 See also North Atlantic
 Treaty Organisation
Atoms for peace M59
Attitudes C77, E36, G11,25,
 39, N29,48,55,72. See also
 Psychological approach to
 international relations
Authority G65, P31,32, R47,

98, S84, T27
Autonomy N15, T29
Aviation X15

Balance of power (Section D)
  A83,89, G90, J11, K13,76,
  107, R84, X5,23
  European C2,18,24,47,51,
  54,78,103,125,131,136
Balfour Declaration C68
Bangladesh K14
Bargaining (Section M) B18,
  25, D16, H38,75, K55,62,
  L20. See also Negotiation
Beck, Colonel Jozef M50
Belgium, colonial policy of
  C115
Belief systems H17. See also
  Ideology
Benedict, Ruth N24
Benes, Eduard M63
Berlin G100
  blockade of R122
  crisis H42, R122
Berthelot, Philippe M10
Beveridge Report J33
Bible P47
Biological warfare J1,38,69
Bipolarity D24,27,36,43, E17,
  K13, X4. See also Polarity
Bismarck, Otto von C125,128,
  G10
Blocs E4, V17,46. See also
  Section D; Alignments, in-
  formal; Alliances
Boer war J95
Bonnet, Georges C1
Boundaries E28,33, N14
  African D3
  disputes H85
Brazil N71
British Commonwealth C48
British Empire C45,112,135
  and Russia C45
Brockdorff-Rantzau, U.K.C.
  C16
Brussels Conference C81
Brussels Treaty C129
Bugeaud, Thomas-Robert K32
Bull, Hedley A69
Bullitt, William C. M38
Bülow, Freiherr Dietrich von
  K85

Bureaucracy C116, G2,63,
  K68, N2, S65
  and foreign policy G93
Burton, John W. H39

Calley, Lt. William P2,11,
  16,18,19,23,35
Cameroons C22,39
Canada C88, D52, G62,103,
  V44
Capitalism J89 U62
Carr, E.H. A50
Case studies A64, G113, H28
Castro, Fidel G14
Catholic Church E34, M30,
  P17, Q17, R117
  and Eastern Europe P17
  and Soviet Union P17
  See also Religion, and
  international relations
Central American Common Mar-
  ket V63
Ceylon E14
Chamberlain, Austen M15
Chamberlain, Neville C1,108,
  M28
Chatham House A68, C133,
  V23
Chicherin, G.V. M42
China (before 1949) D19,
  M62, N25, U10
  foreign policy of M11,35,
  44
  and Japan M22,44, N25
  and United States C12,
  82, M4,5,35,62, N68, P42
China, People's Republic of
  G45,126, U10,35
  decision-making in G40,
  143, K12, L7,21
  foreign policy of D6,29,
  40, G9,45,46,139, M60,
  T49, U36,46, V23
  and international law U10
  and Japan M44
  military policy of K5,40,
  42, L7,21
  politics in G45
  and Soviet Union C73, G56,
  125, U10
  and United States N37,68,
  69, P42
  See also Communism

Cho Fo-hai   M44
Chomsky, Noam   G87
Churchill, Winston S.   K18,30
Ciano, Galeazzo   M27
Civil-military relations   J21,
   22,47,65,72,102, K18
Civil resistance   H67
Civil war   E7, F20, H21,44,
   J45,61,62,80,81, R9,12,21,
   34,35,43,45,71,72,96,99,
   129,131,133,145, S55,66,
   V20. See also Intervention;
   Revolution
Clausewitz, Karl von   H64, J40,
   K86,99
Clemenceau, Georges   C131, K18
Coercion   H81, K13,72, L22,
   Q21, R137, T57. See also
   Force; Power; Violence; War
Coexistence, peaceful   C101,
   D50, H63, Q5,6, R67,93, S17,
   T45, X18. See also Cold war;
   Detente; East-West rela-
   tions; Superpowers
Cold war   A81, C41,66,84,101,
   129, D6,52, G83, H8,14,15,
   19,20,83, J18,81, K84, M39,
   N54,56,57, P44, Q5,6,23,
   R35,101,104,122, S63, T45,
   U5,25, V23. See also
   Coexistence; East-West re-
   lations; Superpowers
Collective mentality   F32, N33.
   See also Psychological as-
   pects of international re-
   lations
Collective security   C59,91,
   D41, H81, K107, P14,55,
   V46. See also Section S
Colonial administration   C3,4,
   13,22,23,30,32,40,42,43,52,
   55,63,75,99,122
Colonialism (Section U)   C2,
   121, F7,41, K32, P32, R48,
   137, S70, T6. See also
   Anti-colonialism; Decolo-
   nisation; History, colonial;
   Imperialism; Neo-colonial-
   ism; Post-colonialism
Colonial policy. See under
   individual countries
Comenius, John Amos   T34
Common markets. See Section V

Commonwealth studies   V45
Communication, international
   (Section N)   C43,80, E5,28,
   F8, G21,25, H39,54,91,92,
   J16, M36, Q1, R49, T6,7,
   V42, X12
Communism   C41, D25, E21, F36,
   G4,6,7,9,17,23,52,124,139,
   H14,55, J89, K76,84, P17,
   50,52, U10,13,21,34,36,46,
   in Africa   F42
   and nationalism   F42
   See also China, People's
   Republic of; Europe, East-
   ern; Marxism; Soviet Union
Comparative method   G110, J17
Comparative politics   G35,130
Concert of powers   D38
Conciliation   R59
Condominium   C98, D38, L26,
   T5
Conference of Paris, 1919
   C119
Conference on Security and
   Cooperation in Europe
   V61,64
Conflict (Section H)   A74,93,
   B1, E35, J4,14,17,37,44,
   60,61,78,80,88,90, K46,80,
   91, M46, N17,73, P4, Q2,3,
   10, 13,14,18, R7,9,35,72,
   116,144
   analysis   A86, D28,59, H3
   behaviour   U18,29
   as a biological concept
   J35,57,68
   and law   R119
   and philosophy   J27,29,71,
   91
   See also Psychology of war
   and conflict; War
Congo, Belgian   C115,136, G72,
   R99,143, S58,80
Congo Conference, Berlin (1885)
   C70
Congo crisis   R99, S58,80
Congress of Vienna, 1815   C119
Congress system, 1815-1825
   C119
Consensus   N33
Content analysis   A32, G145,
   H58,91, N50
Cooperation, economic   C31

Cooperation, international P65, W3,36
Coordination, patterns of R25
Cosmopolitanism S85
Coulondre, Robert M26
Council for Mutual Economic Assistance (COMECON) V38, 52. See also Europe, Eastern
Counter-insurgency J66,104
Crises (Section H) A32, C76, 116, G2,41,57, R52, W29. See also under individual countries
Cuba G14
Cuban missile crisis G14,41, 57,, H60, R53,146
Cultural aspects of international relations F4,8,21, 28, H17,54,77, J67, M60, N32,71, P5,39,64, T35,36, U37, X13
Curzon, Lord C62
Cyprus crisis J4, S41
Czechoslovakia C1, M63

Daladier, Edouard C1
Darwinism M53
Data analysis H24,36,89
Decision-making (Section G) A17,32,34,62,74,87,93, B3, 15, C47,140, D8,13,33, E37, G115, N6, T24,32
 and communication N7,12,23, 46
 in conflict and crisis H1, 30,34,42,58,60,69,72
 defence K4,31,65, N1
 and economics W16,40
 and elites X6
 international B32, H40, R98
 in international organisation S12,13,27,39,40,59, 67,72,77,86, W9
 and public opinion N29,48, 55,57,64,72
 social factors in H24
 in superpowers K59
 and war J14
 See also Policy-making; and under individual countries
Decolonisation C46, E3, H50, R1, S8,45,82. See also

Section U; Anti-colonialism; Colonialism; Postcolonialism
Defence policy (Section K) E16, J65, X23
European V54,64
 of European Economic Community D74, V7,26
 See also Security, national; and under individual countries
Delbrück, Hans K15
Democracy E18,21, J89, R115
Demography R17
Dependence T13
Depression, the C127
Detente D50,59,74, H55,87, L33, R100,101, V7,34. See also Coexistence, peaceful; East-West relations
Determinism H64, P26
Deterrence, nuclear (Section K) D16,55, H43, J16, L9,13,28, 32, M37, P28,40,48, Q22
Development (Section U) D53, F26, G3,37, R1,11,51, S48, T20, V9, W3,26,28,31, 39. See also Modernisation; Third World
Dictatorship G19
Diplomacy (Section M) B4, C6,16,26,28,70,78, D6, G59, H81, K61, N47,71, Q21, S86, V41, W5, X14
Diplomatic history A11, C25
Directed graphs theory D10
Dirksen, Herbert von M55
Disarmament (Section L) D9, J41, Q19, R134, S37,50,53, U32,
 and international organisation R134
 United States K108, L18
 See also Arms control
Diversity R25
Documentation C133
Dodd, William E. M25
Domestic jurisdiction R6, S8,48
Dominican Republic N71
Doob, Leonard H39
Douhet, Giulio K109
Dulles, John Foster G114, H37

Du Picq, Ardent K89

Easter Rising F20
East-West relations C101, D30, N32, P62, R10,66,100,101, V14,28,31,52, W19. See also Coexistence, peaceful; Cold War; Detente; Superpowers
Ecology R124,132. See also Environment, international
Economic and market analogy T40
Economic planning W39
Eden, Anthony C123, H37
Education C43, M14,24,48,49, 56, N16,20,27,55, Q16
Egypt C24,98,121, G134, H37, K50,58, R52, S80, U2
and France C98
and United Kingdom C98
Eisenhower, General Dwight D. C95, H37
Elections and foreign policy G79,138
Elites G1,40,108, N6,10,48, 59, T52, U20,37, X6. See also Leadership
Energy, atomic X4
Energy policy R144
Energy resources V27
Enforcement S58,80
Engels, Friedrich K81
Entente Cordiale C2,47
Environment, international A93, D66, E17, G111,145, H7, N31, R55,124,132, X2. See also Geographical factors in international relations
EOKA-B (Cyprus) J4
Equality of states, doctrine of N32, P63, R48,115,128, S19,23,28
Eritrean Liberation Front J4
Escalation H74,79
Ethics (Section P) See also Morality
Ethiopia J4
Europe, Eastern E4, G56, V36, 38,52
and Catholic Church P17
decision-making in E4
economic studies of V36
and European Community D74
See also Communism; Warsaw Pact
Europe, history of C83,91,98, 135, D35, F15,25,28, G142, Q4
Europe, Western G56,100, V14, 53,64
defence and security of C20,129, D52, K79, V21,31, 41,64
and United States V26
See also Security, European
European common law R123
European Community V10,11,16, 21,28,40,52,61
external relations of V2
See also European Economic Community; Integration, European
European Court of Justice R123
European Economic Community V37,53,56,59,66
and agricultural resources V65
commercial policy of V26
defence policy of D74, V7, V26
and Eastern Europe D74
and energy resources V27
foreign policy of V16
and international economics W32
and Third World U47
and Tunisia V56
and United Kingdom C20
and United States V22,37
See also European Community; Integration, European
European reconstruction C129, G100
Event data analysis A15,30, 49, G50,121
Exchange T3
Exchange rates W24
Expropriation R141

Factor analysis A61, G145
Fanon, Frantz U40
Fante M2

Fascism M27,28,33, N45, P52
Fashoda C103
Federalism E9, T16,39
Federation V48
Feudalism U56
Field theory A47,89, G120
First World War A32, C10,26,
  31,35,57,61,64,65,71,76,85,
  95,105,109,111,112,116,131,
  137,140, H34,35,58,91,92, J10,
  50,53,95, K18, N64. See
  also Sarajevo crisis
Fischer, Fritz C57
Foch, Ferdinand K89
Forbes, W. Cameron M53
Force G18, K6,48,59,82,108,
  R54, U58, V18
  control of R74
  and insurgency H21
  and intervention H21, S70
  military G99, L7,21, T40
  and subversion K100
  and technology K82
  and threats, role of L22
  use of D76, S10
  and violence and social
  change J19
  and war T37
  See also Coercion; Power;
  Violence; War
Force posture K38,57,58. See
  also Defence policy
Ford Foundation E2
Foreign aid C15, G61, N23,
  U1,15,27,28,42,47,52,65,
  W13,34
Foreign policy (Section G)
  A30,75, C60, D34,54,67,
  F35, K26,53, M43, N8,21,23,
  38,66, P13,23,34,47,51, U4,
  12,22,30,37,38,54, V2.
  See also Decision-making;
  Policy-making; and under
  individual countries
Forrester, J.W. A73, D15,47,
  75
France C102, D40, G54,72, K1,
  35,64, N71, R45,52
  African policy of C17,33,
  115,122
  and Algeria C46
  and Anglophobia C17
  colonial policy of C4,18,
  23,30,38,40,43,46,50,60,
  61,75,90,103,122
  decision-making in M10
  and Egypt C98
  foreign office M10
  foreign policy of D68,
  G28,71,97, M9,10,25,26,
  and Germany C83, D67
  military thought of K7,
  28,32,37,47,64,85,89,109
  nationalism in F17
  and United Kingdom C1,2,
  6,7,8,17,20,31,38,47,58,70,
  87,102,103,115,121,127,129,
  131,137
  and United States A80,
  H32
  See also Gaullism
Franco-Soviet Pact, 1935 D68
François-Poncet, André M25
Frederick the Great K85
Freedom P26,31, R47, S84
Freud, Sigmund N17
Functionalism E5, H11, S21,
  30,35,44,51,79,81, T38,39,
  46,51, V4,29,39, W18,27
  See also Neo-functionalism
Futurology C130, G141, R11,
  S20,31, T10,29,55

Gallieni, Joseph-Simon K32
Game theory (Section B) A12,
  14,63,74,91, H10,61,63,64,
  K56,72. See also Simula-
  tion and gaming
Gandhi, Mahatma Q2
Gaullism C20,75, G71,97.
  See also France
General Agreement on Tariffs
  and Trade W9
Geneva Summit Conference,
  1955 C28
Genocide J3,25
Geographical factors in inter-
  national relations E14,20,
  33, X13. See also Environ-
  ment, international;
  Territory
Geopolitics A46, K97,106,109,
  112, R33
George, David Lloyd C48,131,
  K18, M15

Germany (before 1949) C6,16,
 35,51,57,58,64,80,82,100,
 134,140, F25, G53, J50, K30,
 R22,83, U60
 and Africa C13
 colonial policy of C13,22,
 32,55,61,63,71,81,86,99,106,
 112,114,117
 decision-making in C116
 economic policy of C83
 foreign office M16
 foreign policy of M16,18,
 32,55
 and France C83, D67
 imperial policy of C125
 military thought of J20,
 K15,44,81,85,86,99,105,112
 missionary policy of C67
 and nationalism F5,34
 navy of F34
 Nazi C106, M25,26,28
 and Russia C128
 and Soviet Union C134
 and United Kingdom C14,19,
 24,71,78,81,96,112,114,125,
 132,135,136
 See also Hitler, Adolf
Germany, Federal Republic of
 E16, G51,100, K31,35,36,
 R122
 foreign policy of D67, G8,
 10,26,60,85,142, V14
 and Ostpolitik G26, V28
 and proliferation L34
 and Soviet Union D67, G125
 and United Kingdom C96,132,
 D67, G1
 and United States D67, H17
Ghana G72, U11,20
Gold Coast C63, M2, U11
Gorchakov, Alexander Michaelo-
 vich C128
Great powers D1, H57. See
 also Superpowers
Greece, C113, P12
Greeley, Horace F39
Green, Philip K116, P48
Grew, Joseph Clark M1
Grey, Sir Edward M15
Grotius, Hugo P6
Groups, social A22, N10
Guarantees, international
 V15

Guerrilla warfare J66,104
Guibert, Count de K85

Halifax, Lord C1
Hamilton, Alexander K19
Haushofer, Karl K112
Heckscher, E.F. P10
Hegel, G.W.F. P10,59
Henderson, Arthur M61
Henderson, Sir Nevile M28
Herder, Johann Gottfried von
 F28
Herzl, Theodor G67
Hinduism Q20
Hirota Koki M22
Historiography A64, C25,37,
 40,44,74,84,92,104,109,
 117,124, G86,132, J84
History, colonial C4,19,23,
 30,32,33,40,43,51,52,70,
 81,87,90,112,117,122,125,
 136. See also Colonialism;
 Imperialism
History, intellectual C44
History, philosophy of C11,
 P10,26
History, uses of J17
History, world C11
Hitler, Adolf C1,6,14,135,
 F40, J20, M16, U60. See
 also Germany, Nazi
Hollweg, Bethmann C35,57,
 116,140
Hornbeck, Stanley Kuhl M5
Hull, Cordell W2
Human nature A16, Q14, T55.
 See also Aggression;
 Anthropology
Human rights C81, R18,20,
 40,42,47,49,77,112,117,
 130,137, S23
 European law of R41
Hungary C72
Hu Shih M35

Identity T30,48
Ideology (Section P) A60,
 C67, D73, E4,21, G6,7,68,
 128,134,139,144, H17,20,
 55,63, J27,64,89, K13,72,
 N54, P62, T31,45, U8,34,38,

54, X9
Images F32, G4,108. See also
   Section N
Imperial defence C45
Imperialism A83, C3,4,17,18,
   19,22,24,32,38,39,40,42,48,
   50,51,52,55,60,64,67,70,71,
   75,90,103,106,114,115,117,
   136,137, F27, J83, P44,
   R113, S85, U16,21,41.
   See also Colonialism;
   History, colonial; Neo-
   colonialism; Post-colonial-
   ism
Imperialism, economic C33,63,
   87
India K14,57,113, R102, U25
   foreign policy of G70,94
   imperial C45
   and nuclear proliferation
   L3,17
   and Pakistan K57, U29
Individual E37, F16, N35,53,
   P5, Q2
Indo-China G72, R21. See also
   South-East Asia; Vietnam
Indonesia G66, R32
Industrialisation D53, E10,
   J12
Influence D10, G119, J81,
   K72,88, U58. See also
   Power
Integration, European (Section
   V) E17, G30, R123, W1,29.
   See also European Commu-
   nity; European Economic
   Community
Integration, international
   (Section T) A62,64,74,
   D23, E5,11,22,28,30, H4,41,
   N11, S46, V8,11,33,40,42,
   53,59,66, W18,24
Integration, national F5, T21
Integration, political E20,
   N13
Integration, regional (Section
   V) T28,39
Intelligence G41
Inter-Allied Trade Committees
   C111
Inter-American System S11,16,
   V51. See also Latin America
Interdependence D23, E5,15,17,
   30, G60, H9, N14, R25, S26,
   87, T18,28, V16,22, W14,19,
   26,30,32, X6,19
   economic S46, V27, W29,36
   post-colonial C46
Interest groups G18,39,78,136
Internal dissidence E7. See
   also Civil war
Internal-external linkages
   (Section E and G) A55, C2,
   66,76,93,121,125,130,138,
   D17,20,40,53,58, E4,10,14,
   16,20,22,25,26, F6,13,19,
   24,32,33,35, H67,70,90,
   J47,80, K42,111, M15,28,34,
   42, N8,20,21,35,45,47,60,
   61, P12,49, R15,21,34,43,
   45,48,99,105,129,133,145,
   148, S5,48,55, T12,20,23,
   55, U3,4,6,8,10,17,20,29,
   36,45,53,54, V9
International administration
   A31, S33,43,60
International Atomic Energy
   Agency M59, S67
International Court of Justice
   R3,4,24,30,46,58,60,68,70,
   76,82,110
International disputes H19,
   81, R3,59, S31
International economics
   (Section W) C127,140, D21,
   73,74, E10, F8, H6, J10,12,
   50,53,95,101, K19, M3,
   R141, S15,59,77, T6, U6,51,
   V27,37,49,52,56,63, X21
International History
   (Section C) A60, D4,31,52,
   E13, F18,27, G106, J11,83,
   K15,80, M7, N25, P10,26,50,
   Q4, T58, W11, X21
International interaction, re-
   search on H49
International Labour Organi-
   sation R77, S12
International law (Section R)
   A5,55,79, C21,107,139, D2,
   3,17,80, G17, H18,26,65,
   81, J74,88, L1,24, P15,63,
   65, Q10,21, S1,36,52,60,
   64,71,83, T12,22,44,57,58,
   U10,17,31, V47,50, W38.
   See also War, law of

International Law Commission
R30
International Monetary Fund
S77
International monetary system
W8
International order (Section T)
D9,14,49,78, E31, F15,37,
G63, J56,58, L19, N31, P8,
31,53,61, Q1,11,23, R26,38,
44,78,109,114, S6,10,26,46,
U43, X23. See also World
order
International organisation
(Section S) A31,62, C48,
119, D37, E23,37, H1,22,44,
81, M29, N2, R1,8,14,20,21,
27,34,43,44,45,51,72,73,76,
79,80,92,99,104,115,120,
133,134,138, 143,145, T22,
47,50, U57, V17,19,46,47,50,
63, W3,4,8,13,15,39
International police R105
International relations, methodology of (Sections A and B)
C5,25,37,92,104,124, D45,48,
66,70,75,79, E32, G3,87,110,
113,114,115, H39,45,49,71,
74,80, J39,63,75,84,85,87,
96, K34,67, N5,28,42,59, T7,
9,32,53, V1,53, W16,29,37
International relations, study
of (Sections A and B) C84,
133, D18,34,48, E25,26,
F30, G34,86,109,132,140,
J8, K47,56,75,86, L2,25,
N28,34,50, P21,43,57,60,
Q12,13, R73,109, T11,18,56,
V45,53,62, W28,37
International relations,
theory of (Sections A and B)
D17,48,51,64,79,80, E22,
F30, G44,60,112, H68, J61,
63, N14, P12,29,55,57,60,
R103, S5, T2,9,38, U3,8,53,
V25,60
conflict Q13
decision-making D33, E37,
G115
deterrence K34, P28,48
international law R109
International settlement J62
International system (Section
D) A16,46,55,71,75, B6,

C7,20,29,54,94,102,129,
131,137, E8,13,15,17,19,
23,25,27,31,35,37, F14,
G3,47,61,90,91, H9,16,80,
J16,17,45,61,74,79,80,81,
K2,6,46,71,76,115, L19,26,
M20,41,52, N26,34,59, P6,8,
20,29,33,47,53,61,66, Q11,
R1,37,38,46,65,75,78,84,
97,115,120,131, S15,31,35,
37,54,55,56,87, T2,3,5,9,
11,13,16,20,26,40,47,50,
57,58,59, U7,18,39,45,49,
54,59,66, V10,20,24, W14,
30,31, X3,6,9,19,23
1817-1945 L2
to 1870 C5
to 1914 T33
1870-1914 C126, K69, N64
1919-1939 C1,3,6,14,30,
39,58,91,120,123,127,135,
T33
1919-1970 M8
1945-1970 G88, H32, J13,
K43,49, S15, U23,64, V30,
W25, X4
See also Systems analysis
and theory
International Telecommunication Union S39
Internationalism N74, S85
Intervention C107,139, D17,
26,42, G17,44,104,112, H21,
J61, K100, P61, R13,14,21,
34,43,45,50,92,99,103,129,
133,145,148, S5,66, U3,10,
See also Civil war
Iramba C93
Iran, and Soviet Union C97
Ireland J4
and United Kingdom F20
Islam F1, G134, P20,29,50,66,
U38,54. See also Middle
East; Religion, and international relations
Isolationism C29,59, N40,
P55. See also United States,
foreign policy of
Israel C121, K39,50,58, L3,
R86. See also Arab-Israeli
war, 1967; Zionism
Italy C49, D31, E16, M18,27,
28,33
Fascism in M27,28,33

163

and United Kingdom C51

Japan E14,16, G88.,124, K111,
   R19
   and China M22,44, N25
   foreign policy of C89, M3,
   12,13,22,34,57, N25,
   and internal politics G95
   naval strategy of K60
   and nuclear proliferation
   L3,38
   and Soviet Union M13
   and United States C89, M1,
   5,12,53, N6,24,44,60, P41
Johnson, Nelson Trusler M62
Joint Defence Arrangements
   C91
Jomini, Henri K7,47
Judaism F1
Justice H13, R127,128
Just war. See War, just

Kahn, Herman H64, N24
Kant, Immanuel J18, P59
Kaplan, Morton A. A45, D70
Kashmir R102
Kellogg Pact C27
Kelsen, Hans R69
Kennan, George A46
Kennedy, John F. R53
Kennedy, Joseph P. M38
Kenya M40
Khrushchev, Nikita K87
King, Mackenzie D52
Kitchener, Lord C85
Koo, V.K. Wellington M11
Korea R19
Korean War H60
Kuwait Agreement C62

Language J59, N30,39, S34,
   T35, V57
Lasswell, Harold D. A18, N28,
   34,50
Latin America G14, S11,16,
   U33,56, V9,42,44,51,63
   and United States H77,
   V44,63
   See also Inter-American
   System

Law, natural P36
Leadership E37, F40, G14,19,
   43,63,65,67,76,108,114,
   133,135, M6, T15
   and foreign policy D20,
   E4
   revolutionary S32
   and totalitarianism G16
   in war K18
   See also Elites
League of Nations C4,39,48,
   58,59,61,91,106,118,119,
   G57, M11,45, R77,134, S21,
   27,45,54,61,74,78,83. See
   also Mandate system
League of Neutrals C49
Léger, Alexis Saint-Léger M9
Legitimacy D64, E21, F16,
   G65, R7,54,70, V11
Lenin, V.I. K20, P62
Leopold II of Belgium C115
Liberalism C77, G84
Liddell Hart, Basil K28
Limited war J16,61,80, K4,52,
   55,62,94,95,102,114.
   See also War
List, Friedrich K19
Litvinov, Maxim M51
Lloyd, Henry Humphrey Evans
   K47
Locarno Treaties C58,120
Locke, John P37
London School of Economics
   A24
Loyalty, world T31
Ludendorff, Erich K105
Lyautey, Louis-Hubert-Conzalve
   K32

Machiavelli, Niccolo A17,
   K29, P15
Mackinder, Halford J. A46
Mackinnon Agreement C24
MacMurray, John Van Antwerp
   M4
Maginot, André K28
Maginot Line K28
Mahan, Alfred Thayer A46,
   K106
Maji Maji rebellion C55
Malaysia R32
Mandate system C4,39,48,61,

71,106,118. See also League
of Nations
Manning, C.A.W. T2
Mao Tse-tung G44, K12, T49
Marx, Karl K81, P62
Marxism J89,92,97, P62, X7.
See also Communism
Mass communication. See Communication, international;
News media
Mass politics F25
Mass psychology N31
Materialism T54
Matsuoka Yosuke M34,57
McGowan, Patrick J. G93
Mediation Q12, R59
Mediterranean C24,137, V26
Middle East C62,68,85,121, F1,
10, G24, H37,57, J37, K39,
50,58, R86, V15,35
and Soviet Union V35
and United States V12
See also Islam
Military aid L18, U1,65
Military doctrines and thinking (Section K). See also
Strategy; War; and under
individual countries
Military expansion C60
Military ideology K2,14
Military-industrial complex
J101, K54,67,68
Military organisation K17
Military planning C31
Military reserves J22
Military, sociology of J43
Military technology K77, L36
Minorities F23, G37
Mitchell, William K109
Mobilisation, industrial J95
Model-building A36,40,57,77,
B21,28, D47,75, H46, R84,
T53
Modernisation R11, T20, U3,
53, X9. See also Development; Third World
Moltke, Helmuth von K44
Morality (Section P) A81, J3,
16,36, K48, Q22
and disarmament L15
international J5, Q1
and nuclear war J5,84
personal/private D15, J15,

28,30,48,100
political/public J9,18,25,
48,54,100, N15, R47
and strategy K77
and war J3,9,30,73,100,
103, R108
Moroccan crisis C78
Morocco V56
Multinational corporations
E10,18, N63, R80, W12,14,
18,20,21,23,30. See also
Transnationalism
Munich crisis C1,108
Mussolini, Benito M33
Mutual Balanced Force Reduction L33
My Lai massacre P2,3,11,16,
18,19,23,35. See also
Vietnam War

Napoleonic and Revolutionary
wars J12
Nasser, Abdel Gamel C121,
H37, U2
Nation and nation-state
(Sections E and F) A71,
D32, J56, T30, V8,11,24,
30, W20
Nationalism (Section F) A21,
E9, H38,41,86, M11, N71,
74, P10,42, R25,48,107,
S85, T14,16, U11,43,63,
V30, X15. See also under
individual countries
Nationality F23, N51,65
National attributes and foreign policy G29,82, H27
National character F9,21,22,
H54,71
National culture F21, H54
National interest A60, G36,
144, J29, K107, L39, P21,
30,41,51,56, R35
National and international
politics, comparison of
K72
National liberation, wars of
S70, U10
National security. See Security,
national
National socialism F25, U60.
See also Germany (before 1949)

National stereotypes   Q16
National values   J28
Natural law.   See Law, natural
Natural right   P36
Naumann, Friedrich   F34
Navies
   German   F34
   Soviet   K90
   United Kingdom   J65
   United States   K90
   See also Sea power
Nazi-Soviet Pact, 1939   C134
Negotiation (Section M)   C134, H75, J62, S3.   See also Bargaining
Neo-colonialism   U21,34,44,59. See also Colonialism; Imperialism; Post-colonialism
Neo-functionalism   V49. See also Functionalism
Neurath, Konstantin von   M16
Neutralism   U48,50,54,57. See also Non-alignment
Neutrality   C91, D71, N45, R23, U2,5,46,48
News media   C82, G21, N3,19, 38,72. See also Communication, international
New states, role of   D37
Niebuhr, Reinhold   P43
Nigeria   M40
Nile   C24
Nkrumah, Kwame   U11
Nomura Kichisaburo   M12
Non-alignment   U5,6,9,25,44, 48,61. See also Neutralism
Non-governmental organisations   E2,29,34
Non-violence   H67, Q16, T57. See also Violence
Nordic area.   See Scandinavia
Normative theory   A18,63, E27, G77, J29,91, P7,21,57, T17, 44
North Atlantic Treaty Organisation   C20,88,129, D52,56, K9,64,79, 87, L33,34, P12, V4,21,31,41. See also Alliances; Blocs
North-South relations   D30, U31, V10,14, W10
Norway   G39
Nuclear deterrence.   See Deterrence, nuclear
Nuclear war.   See War, nuclear
Nuclear weapons.   See Weapons, nuclear
Nuremburg trials   R22,83. See also War crimes
Nyasaland   C99

Oceans policy   R16,55
Oil crisis, significance of   W37
Open Door policy (China)   C12, M5. See also United States, and China
Oppenheim, Lassa   P6
Opposed systems analysis   A87
Organisation of African Unity   S7
Organisation of American States   S11,16, V51
Organisation theory   A79
Ottoman Empire   C85
Outer space   R106,140

Pacific area   C34,89
Pacifism.   See Section Q
Pakistan   E20, K14,57, R102
   and India   K57, U29
Palestine   C68
Pan-Slavism   F36, G23
Papacy.   See Catholic Church
Parliament, United Kingdom   G105
Parties, political   G105, T41
Peace (Section Q)   A80, C21, D22, J47, L22, P7,59, R24, 107,130,136, S17,20,63, T45, X7,18
   making   C10
   movement   E12, G80
   plans for   H51
   research   B32, H3, R87
   as a universal goal   C101, J14,34,35,57, L11, S26
   See also War
Peaceful change   R1,137, S6, 24,48, T43
Peaceful coexistence.   See Coexistence, peaceful
Peaceful settlement   R77
Peace-keeping, international

N18, Q12, R134, S18,24,41,
42,50,53,58,75,76,80,82.
See also United Nations
Pearson, Lester D52
Perception A71, D64, G4,108,
145, H8,10,15,32,34,42,58,
76,84, N53,54,56,59,68,69,
73, P44, T15,49. See also
Psychological approach to
international relations
Persian Gulf C62
Personality A19, B15, G14,133,
H37, K65, N2,18. See also
Psychological approach to
international relations
Perth, Earl of M28
Philosophy, methodology of
P7
Planning G92, J33
Polar regions R113
Polarity T40. See also Bipolarity
Polemology H3
Policy application A39, P28
Policy-making (Section G) A17,
34,86, C77,84, K42, N22,56,
58. See also Decision-making; Foreign policy
Policy research G59, K96
Political change U66
Political community, growth of
X8
Political-military doctrine
K39,45
Political philosophy (classical) K13, P60
Political systems, types of
G68, T59
Population D21, J15,52,98,
R17, X9
Portugal, and Africa C136
Positivism A63
Post-colonialism E3, U49. See
also Neo-colonialism
Poverty R56, U31
Power
concept of D23,55,61,77,
E6,21, H9, K63
and ethics P47
in international relations
theory A12,19,52,54,60,62,
79, R120
military D65, G99, K48,63,
72,76,84, M41, P13, R140,
T40
nuclear D25,39, K24,25,
R144, T1
politics D22, P64
of small states D5,7, E35
and world order T8,13,40
See also Coercion; Force;
Influence; Violence; War
Prescriptive study T17. See
also Normative theory
Pressure, physical M43
Prestige J99, L5, Q6
Private armies J74
Progress P32, T58
Project Michelson K75
Project Temper B1
Proliferation, nuclear
(Section L) D39, G58, K3,
11,51, M52
Propaganda (Section N) J81,
M43, P50, X12
Protest U62
Provisional I.R.A. J4
Psychiatry N62
Psychoanalysis G19,67
Psychological approach to
international relations
(Section N) H76,78, J46,
63, Q14, T14,31,52. See
also Attitudes; Collective
mentality; Perception;
Personality; Propaganda
Psychology (Section N) A38,
39, C74, F3, G65, H86, J39,
84, L13, P49, T30,54
of war and conflict H8,14,
J32,46,70, Q5
Public opinion (Section N)
A61, C70, E36, F9, G18,42,
78,107, H66, J2,8, L16,
V32
Purpose T36

Quantification A2,13,32,92,
93, B5, D60, J86, K34
Quarantine, Cuban. See Cuban
missile crisis
Quebec E7
Quemoy crisis H47

Race (Section F) Q16
Radicalism H50
Radio Liberty N61
Rationality A53, G77,135, H61,
   J29, K91,116, N17,29, S26
Realism K72, P21,22, S26
Realpolitik A83
Red Cross R112
Regionalism (Section V) F10,
   G134, K107, P66, R126, S3,
   7,16,32, T29
Religion, and international
   relations C67,90, E34, F10,
   25, J103, M30, P20,43,47,
   58, Q17,20, R117, U38. See
   also Catholic Church; Islam
Renaissance city-states,
   Italian D31
Research problems H49, K67
Reserve Officer Training Corps
   J72
Resources H12, R16,49,55, X21
Revolution E1, J4,90, R38,129,
   S32, T12,20. See also Civil
   war
Rhineland crisis C6
Rhodesia S45
Ribbentrop, Joachim von M16
Richardson, Lewis F. H64
Ritter, Gerhard C57
Roosevelt, Franklin Delano
   K30
Rosenau, James N. G74,82,93
Rousseau, Jean-Jacques F28
Rumbold, Sir Horace M25
Russia
   and British Empire C45
   foreign policy of C54,138,
   G23,98,133, K26, M17, N4,
   W41
   and Germany C128
   history of C11,54, F36,
   G13,20,23,98,106,133, K26
   M17, W41
   See also Soviet Union

Salisbury, Lord C45,62
Sarajevo crisis H34,35,36,
   58,89,92. See also First
   World War
Sartre, Jean-Paul U40
Scandinavia C91, F43, K83,
   S69, V6. See also indivi-
   dual countries
Schlieffen, Count Alfred K44
Schulenberg, Friedrich Werner
   M55
Science and technology
   (Section X) D9, G4, H12,
   J53,67, K8,10,37,77,82,96,
   109, L36,37, R16,81,95,140,
   T34, U64, W11
Sea power K97,106. See also
   Navies
Second World War C7,8,10,15,
   72,75,79,83,100,102,108,
   109,137, J20,33, K30, M12,
   13,22,39,57, R22
Secrecy G35
Security H66, J21, K107, V31
   community V6
   European C1,58,127, K79
   national D30, K96,104,
   X10
   systems V4
   See also Defence policy;
   Europe, Western, defence
   and security of
Seeley, Sir John F27
Self-determination, national
   C131, F2,7,12,15, H13,41,
   P52, R62, S70
Seversky, Alexander de K109
Shidehara, Kijuro M3
Shigemitsu Mamoru M13
Simulation and gaming
   (Section B) A62, D11, H30,
   69,72, K93. See also Game
   theory
Slave trade C81
Smith, Adam K19
Social change D21, J19, U54,
   X16
Social Darwinism C64
Socialism J83
Social Science (Sections A
   and B) D8, G87,107, H13,
   51,53,88,
Societal values H66
Sociology of international
   relations H2, N10, Q7
Solf, Wilhelm C86
Sombart, Werner P10
South Africa C19,118,135,
   F38, G89,101, S45. See

also Apartheid; South West
  Africa
South Asia   K14. See also
  Asia
South-East Asia   G52, J13,66,
  V39. See also Asia; Indo-
  China; Vietnam
Sovereignty (Section E)   A88,
  F2, J45,62, K13, P65, R2,
  35,94,97,113,115, S82, T33,
  V8,40, W20,23,33,43. See
  also State
South West Africa   C13,118
Soviet Union   C16,73,134, D6,
  25,59, F23, G120, H8, J97,
  K1,6,66,70,110, M26, N61,
  71, Q7, R59,122, U34,36,46,
  V36,38
  and Africa   V13
  and Catholic Church   P17
  and China, People's Repub-
    lic of   C73, G56,125, U10
  and communism   G7
  decision-making in   M51
  defence policy of   G56,
    K16,25,70,71,87,110,114,
    115, L4
  and deterrence   K23
  Far Eastern policy, studies
    of   V23
  foreign policy of   C28,41,
    D68, F36, G4,5,6,17,20,24,
    40,56,96,99,106,125,128,
    M18,42,51, P50, R10,66,
    U14, V34,64, W34
  and Germany   C134, D67,
    G125
  history of   C54, K20
  and international law   G17,
    R67,93
  and international system
    C54, D43
  and Iran   C97
  and Japan   M13
  law reform in   R10
  and Middle East   V35
  military thought of   K20,
    23,66,70,114
  nationalities in   F23
  Navy   K90
  outlook of   N73
  in Second World War   C72
  and totalitarianism   G16

  and United States   G56,
    H37,55,87, K13,87, M58,59,
    R146, X7
  and use of force   K59
  See also Cold War; Commu-
    nism; East-West relations;
    Superpowers; Warsaw Pact
Spanish-American War   C12
Spain   R133
Spengler, Oswald   P10
Spykman, Nicholas J.   A46
Stability, international
  D49, J86, K51, U49
Stalin, Joseph V.   G19, K30
State (Section E)   A85, D5,7,
  14,46,61, E22, F26, R61,
  92, S1, T1,33, W31. See
  also Sovereignty
Statecraft   M43
Statistical analysis. See
  Quantification
St. Laurent, L.S.   D52
Strategic Arms Limitation
  Talks   L33. See Arms con-
  trol
Strategic Studies   J21, K23
Strategic weapons. See
  Weapons, nuclear
Strategy (Sections K and L)
  A64, C20,31, H61,62,64,
  M37,41, P28,40, X1,3.
  See also War
Stratification, international
  G127, H16, U33,56
Stresemann, Gustav   C120, G53
Submarine warfare   K90
Subversion   K100
Sudan, Western   C60, M31
Suez Canal   C24
Suez crisis   C121, H37, R52,
  S58,80
Summit conferences   M39
Superpowers   D1,6,20,29,38,
  50,54,55,63, L26, S42, T5,
  U24. See also Coexistence;
  Cold War; East-West rela-
  tions; Soviet Union;
  United States
Supra-nationalism   V24
Survey data   A61, N42
Survey of International
  Affairs   C133
Sweden   L6,35, M45

Switzerland V48
Symbols H79, N28,36,74, T36
Systems analysis and theory
 (Section A) D19,31,33,44,
 45,47,51,62,70,79, G2,38,
 H24,48, J14,60, K56, Q13,
 V57. See also International
 system

Tanganyika C3
Tanzania C93, G127
Taylor, A.J.P. C125
Technology. See Section X
Tension reciprocation L28
Territorial disputes H13
Territory H85, K80,107, X15.
 See also Geographical factors in international relations
Terrorism, international J4,
 37,44,78,88, P4
Third World (Section U) C46,
 F10,42, G66,70,127,144,
 H50, P32, R1,19,28,31,48,
 129, S29,41,48,59,62, T20,
 29, V13,20, W12,26,28,33.
 See also Development;
 Modernisation
Threat H43, K49, Q3,18, T3
 perception C91, H36,89,
 N53
Togo C63
Tolstoy, Leo H64
Totalitarianism G16, J20,
 M18
Tradition, role in foreign
 policy G10,36
Transaction analysis T19,
 V55
Transnationalism D61, E2,17,
 19,22,23,29,34,36, G23,
 R80, S44, W38,40,42. See
 also Multinational corporations
Transvaal C19
Treaties C94,97, D2, L29,
 R118,139
Trotsky, Leon K20
Truman Doctrine C113
Trusteeship C4,86
Tunisia C38, V56
 and European Economic Community V56
Turkey C65, M19

Uganda C56, G129, M40, U20
Unconditional surrender K30
Undén, Östen M45
UNESCO S72
United Kingdom E14, F11,27,
 J33, K2,9,27,35,36, R52,
 102, U60
 and Africa C33,115,122
 Cabinet G12
 Colonial Office C52
 colonial policy of C3,4,
 17,18,24,32,38,39,42,43,
 50,52,60,63,70,71,81,87,
 99,103,106,114,117,122
 decision-making in M15
 defence policy of J10,53,
 95, K78
 and Egypt C98
 and European Economic Community C20
 Foreign Office M15
 foreign policy of C14,24,
 48,58,62,68,78,91,94,112,
 D54,57, G137, K78, M15,25,
 28,47,61, N19, V14, W7,22,
 43
 and France C1,2,6,7,8,17,
 20,31,38,47,58,70,87,102,
 103,115,121,127,129,131,
 137
 and Germany C14,19,24,71,
 78,81,96,112,114,125,132,
 135,136, D67, G1
 imperial policy C45
 interest groups in G137
 and Ireland F20
 and Italy C51
 military thought of K2,9,
 27,28
 missionary policy of C67
 and nationalism F11
 Parliament of G105
 Royal Navy J65
 Treasury G32
 and United States C12,20,
 89,112, D54, H37
United Nations (Section S)
 C139, D37, H1,22, M29, N2,
 P22, R8,15,20,23,27,28,30,

31,39,40,46,48,52,58,60,73,
76,77,96,102,104,106,131,
137,139.143,148, T22, U5,
57, V17,47
and Arab-Israeli conflict
R86
Charter of R33,134,138
General Assembly R60, S2,
86
Secretariat S65
Secretary General S27
Security Council S24
Specialised Agencies R51,
79, S33,51,81
and the Third World S62
Trusteeship system U55
and United States P14,
S25
See also Peace-keeping,
international; and specialised agencies
United Nations Economic Commission for Latin America
V42
United States C126, D6,25,59,
F39, G106,126, J55, K1,79,
N66,71, Q7,15, R21,52,122,
145, S11,16, V10,44,51,63
alliance policy D56, G61
and Asia C34,89, P41, V23
and China C12,82, M4,5,35,
62, N37,68,69, P42
decision-making in C29,66,
G104,136, J48, L40, N47,72,
P30, V63, W2, X11
defence policy of C9, G2,
K53,61,65,73,74,76,84,95,
104, L4,23,31,39, N58
Department of State H42,
N47
and disarmament K108, L18
domestic politics in G55,
Q8
and Europe C129, V26
and European Economic Community V22,37
foreign policy of C9,15,
21,27,28,29,34,59,66,69,77,
84,113,130, D12, F13,19,24,
31,33,35, G27,41,52,55,61,
73,76,83,84,86,104,107,120,
123,132, H42,79, J3,13,28,
36,48,60, K17,108, M1,4,5,

23,25,38,39,53,60,62, N23,
25,35,44,45,47,59, P24,30,
34,37,42,49,51,56, R15,53,
107,143, S78, U15,41,66,
V12,41, W2,34, X10,11,13
and France A80, H32
and Germany D67, H17
and Greece C113
immigration policy of
C110
in international economy
W40
and international law
R93
and international organi-
sation P55
and international system
D43
and Japan C89, M1,5,12,
53, N6,24,25,44,60, P41
and Latin America H77,
V44,63
and League of Nations
P14
and Middle East V12
military thought of J55,
K61,95,106,109,116
national interest of L39
nationalism in F39
Navy K90
outlook of F32, N73
presidency G55,73
propaganda strategy of
N36
public opinion in N56
and Second World War C102,
,155
Senate G114
and Soviet Union G56, H37,
55,87, K13,87, M58,59,
R146, X7
and United Kingdom C12,
20,89,112, D54, H37
and United Nations P14,
S25
and use of force K59
and world peace P14,55
See also Isolationism;
North Atlantic Treaty
Organisation; Superpowers
Universal Declaration of
Human Rights R47. See
also Human rights

Values (Section P) A5,56,
  C64, D15, G27, H7,66, K48,
  N8,36,66, T24,36,44,48,52,
  U35
Vatican. See Catholic Church
Vauban, Sébastien le Prestre
  de K37
Versailles Treaty C131. See
  also First World War
Vietnam J3,104, R21. See also
  Indo-China; South-East Asia
Vietnam War H79,84, J36,48,
  60,100, P2,3,11,16,18,19,
  23,25,35, X1
Violence H16,23, Q9, R7. See
  also Coercion; Force;
  Non-violence; Power; War

War (Sections J and K) A80,
  C26,27,53,92,109, D41,65,
  F2, G47, H3,23,81,83, Q3,
  7,10,14,21, R39,90, T4,8,
  X13,21,22
  and balance of power D27
  and economics C83,111,140,
  W11
  and force T37
  just J73, P6, U10
  law of R9,21,23,34,39,43,
  45,83,86,90,99,108,112,131,
  133,145
  and legal responsibility
  P2,3,
  mobilisation for J22
  and moral responsibility
  P2,3,6,16,18,19,23,35,59
  nuclear D30, N1, P54, Q22,
  R108, T4, X1
  and social anthropology
  H59
  undeclared G136
  See also Coercion; Conflict;
  Force; Limited war; Peace;
  Power; Psychology of war
  and conflict; Violence;
  Weapons; and under individual wars
War crimes P2,3,11,18,27,
  R22,83
Warsaw Pact G56, L33. See
  also Europe, Eastern;
  Soviet Union

Washington Conference C89
Weapons
  acquisition of K1,5,22,
  36,41,50,54,113,
  conventional L1
  nuclear D11,13,16, J16,
  41,42,84,103, K8,11,43,52,
  53,62,77,87,92,94, L39,
  P1,54, R144, V7,41, X9,10,
  17
  See also Armaments; War
Welfare, human R49,56,79.
  See also Section W;
  Development
Wells, H.G. E10
Western society U62
Westphalia, Peace of R33
Wilson, Woodrow C48,77,131,
  M23
World federation X23
World Health Organisation
  S40
World order (Section T) N3,
  P9, R129,147, S20,60, U33,
  55, W35, X17. See also
  International order
World society/community
  (Section T) A89, E12,
  J26, M21, Q7, R11,98, S30.
  See also International
  order; World order
World state F11
World War I. See First World
  War
World War II. See Second
  World War
Wright, Quincy A43,44,47,78

Yemen R12

Zionism F1, G67. See also
  Israel
Zollverein V54

Ref
Z
6461
W7